Modern Simple

GLUTEN-FREE INSTANT POT COOKBOOK

Effortless and Convenient Recipes that the Entire Family Will Enjoy—Even Individuals without Gluten Sensitivity!

JANE BONACCI &
SARA DE LEEUW

NEW SHOE PRESS

Quarto.com

First Published in 2022 by New Shoe Press, an imprint of The Quarto Group,
100 Cummings Center, Suite 265-D, Beverly, MA 01915, USA.
T (978) 282-9590 F (978) 283-2742

ISBN: 978-0-7603-9546-2

The content in this book was previously published in *The Gluten-Free Instant Pot Cookbook* (The Harvard Common Press, 2019) and *Quick and Easy Gluten-Free Instant Pot Cookbook* (New Shoe Press, 2022) by Jane Bonacci and Sara De Leeuw.

Photography: Kristin Teig

Printed in China

Contents

Why Use a Pressure Cooker?

There is a certain satisfaction in having dinner simmering away on the stove, filling the house with delicious smells. But what if there were a way to have that same dinner in a fraction of the time? With today's busy schedules and so many people on the go, using an electric pressure cooker can be a game-changer.

Let's walk through some basic information about electric pressure cookers and review some of the tools you'll want to have on hand to be successful.

Pressure cookers have several benefits over more traditional cooking methods. Here are some of the top reasons to use a pressure cooker:

Exceptional flavor and nutrition! How food is prepared matters! Pressure cookers create a depth of flavor in your dishes like no other cooking method. They help retain the quality of the foods you cook by preparing them quickly and with very little water. Heat is distributed swiftly, allowing flavor to penetrate into your food more deeply than with traditional cooking. The steam inside the pot allows meats to become moist and succulent and vegetables to retain their crispness, beautiful color, and, most importantly, their flavor. Vitamins and nutrients are better retained in foods cooked with a pressure cooker because they are cooked for a shorter amount of time. Less time means less opportunity for vitamins and minerals to be dissolved away, making food healthier and better for you.

Food cooks quickly! In a pressure cooker, the cooking time is greatly reduced. You can cook foods up to 70 percent faster than other conventional methods. This is a handy feature when you're trying to get dinner on the table in a short amount of time. You don't have to spend hours at the stove any longer. Because food is cooked so quickly, it still retains all the richness and natural flavors of foods cooked for hours in the oven. (See above.) You can make a pot of beans, a whole chicken, soups and stews, roasts, and rice so quickly and easily that the pressure cooker will be your new best friend in the kitchen.

They are safe! Electric pressure cookers are much safer than your grandmother's (or mother's) pressure cooker. Today's designs have numerous built-in safety features that ensure safe, successful meals without fear of the exploding pressure cookers of yesteryear. The pressure, heating, and sealing functions are all regulated, so you don't have to worry. Lids must be locked in place before pressure builds and won't open until pressure has been released.

They use less energy! Electric pressure cookers take far less energy than cooking with multiple pots on your stovetop or hours in your oven. This can be a significant savings. With much less water used in cooking, it is also better for the environment. Because foods are cooked in far less time, less energy is needed to prepare meals. An added bonus? Electric pressure cookers won't heat up the kitchen when you use them.

Cleanup is a breeze! Cook in one pot and clean one pot. It doesn't get any easier. Cooking on your stovetop can leave splatters across your counters and walls, resulting in extra mess and more to clean. With an electric pressure cooker, everything is contained, and most of the time, you'll have only one pot and the lid to clean. And less mess means even less time spent in the kitchen. You'll have more time to spend with your kids or doing the things you love.

How Do Pressure Cookers Work?

A pressure cooker is a sealed pot with a valve that controls the steam and pressure inside the pot. Pressure cookers work by heating liquids in a tightly sealed pot, which creates steam. As the liquid boils, the trapped steam raises the internal cooking temperature past the boiling point of water. The internal temperature of the pot can reach upwards of 250°F (120°C). The higher heat, and conversely higher pressure, forces liquid into the food and cooks it much faster than traditional methods. In fact, foods can be cooked up to 70 percent faster in a pressure cooker. Pressure-cooked foods become moist, juicy, and succulent. Tough fibers break down faster, so inexpensive cuts of meat become fork-tender in a very short amount of time. Dried beans don't need to be soaked for hours, and you can cook healthy, nutritious alternative grains in minutes.

The Parts of a Pressure Cooker

Though there are many different brands of electric pressure cookers on the market, they all have similar features. Here are some of the basics you'll find on every model:

Outer Housing Unit or Base: This is what holds the inner cooking pot. The display/control panel will be located on the outside. The control panel is where you will program your pressure cooker to cook. It will have all the function buttons and any preset programs. On the inside of the housing unit is the heating element. This is located at the base of the unit and looks like a ceramic disk. At the center of the heating element is a temperature sensor. The temperature sensor does just that—senses the temperature of your pressure cooker. It will automatically shut off if it senses the temperature inside the pot is too high.

Inner Cooking Pot: This is where the magic happens! Most brands have removable inner pots that are made of stainless steel, ceramic, or aluminum. These are almost all dishwasher safe, and that makes cleanup simple and easy! Always make sure your inner pot is in the housing unit before adding any liquid or ingredients to your pressure cooker. Some inner pots will have a "Max" fill line etched on the inside. This is another safety system for pressure cookers and ensures the food inside doesn't bubble up too far and clog the valves.

Lid: The lid of your pressure cooker is where you'll find the majority of safety features and all the cooking valves.

Pressure Release Valve: This is sometimes called a steam release handle, pressure limit valve, or pressure regulator knob. It is used to control the pressure inside your cooker. Generally, there are two positions for this valve. There is a "sealing" or "pressure" position. This is the position your pressure release valve should be in every time you begin cooking. It will seal in the steam and allow the pressure to build so you can cook food successfully. There is also a "venting" position, used after the cook time is complete to allow the built-up steam to escape. Occasionally these positions are marked on the exterior of the lid, but not always. When you release pressure from a pressure cooker, be aware that very hot steam is being expelled from your machine at a high rate. At no time should you put your face or hands near this steam. Burns from hot steam are quite painful, and we don't want you to get hurt.

Float Pin or Float Valve: This is one of the safety features on a modern electric pressure cooker. A tiny valve located on the lid of your appliance, it resembles a flat nail head. This valve gets pushed up by the steam inside your pot when the unit comes to pressure. The valve helps seal the cooker and prevents the lid from being opened while at pressure. When the float pin drops, it means the majority of pressure has escaped from the pot and you can safely open the lid.

Sealing Ring: Also called a rubber gasket or silicone gasket, this removable ring is found under the lid of your pressure cooker. It's made of stiff food-grade silicone and forms a pressure-tight seal between the lid and the pressure cooker. This is removable, so you can take it out to clean it. Gaskets should be replaced every year or if they develop a thin spot.

The Display Buttons on the Control Panel

The display buttons on different brands, models, and sizes of electric pressure cookers all have their own functions. Each of those functions makes them unique and special. Many have programs built in for things like soup, grains, meats, eggs, or even cakes. When using these function buttons, the pressure cooker will cook for a specific amount of time at a specific pressure. The time and pressure settings cannot be changed. There is a simple convenience to being able to push a button and walk away. Know, too, that the pressure cooker can't tell what type of food is in the pot. If you use the "Poultry" button for cooking rice because you like how it turns out, no one will ever know.

Every pressure cooker will also have an option for setting the cooking time manually. It may be a button that actually says "Manual," or it might be labeled as something else. Get to know this button on your electric pressure cooker! Many recipes, including all the ones in this book, are written with instructions to "Press Manual and cook for XX minutes." This allows everyone the flexibility to use the same recipes, regardless of the brand or model of pressure cooker you own.

The "Sauté" or "Browning" button allows you to sear food before cooking it. This button works best for searing meats or sautéing vegetables. You can also use this function after cooking to thicken sauces and gravies. Some brands have a "Simmer" option, which you can use in any recipe that doesn't require the higher heat point of sautéing.

There will be a "Cancel/Keep Warm" button. This button will cancel any function currently in progress or simply turn off your pressure cooker. The "Keep Warm" part of the button allows you to keep food inside your cooker warm after the end of the cooking time. Some pressure cookers will let you decide whether you want to keep foods warm or have the cooker automatically shut off at the end of the cooking time. Read your manual to know whether your electric pressure cooker has this option.

Some pressure cookers feature multiple pressure settings, so you can choose to cook at high pressure or low pressure. Usually that setting is changed with + or - buttons located on the control panel.

Your electric pressure cooker will have a display timer that allows you to set the amount of time needed to cook. It will count down once the pot is at pressure and will show you how much cooking time is left before the food is done.

A locking lid is one of the most important safety features of modern electric pressure cookers. The lid cannot be removed while the pot is under pressure. If for some reason something were to go wrong with your pressure cooker, such as the valves were blocked or the electricity were to go out, your lid would remain locked until the pressure inside had decreased enough for the unit to be opened safely. Remember those horror stories about exploding pots and scraping food off the ceiling? This is likely because the lid was forced open on the pressure cooker without properly releasing the inside pressure. Locking lids mean today's electric pressure cookers don't have this problem.

Pressure Release Methods

There are three ways to release the pressure inside your electric pressure cooker: a quick release method, a natural release method, and a combination of the two.

Quick Pressure Release Method, or "QPR": This is when you release all the steam immediately after the cooking time ends. Do this by opening the steam handle to the "venting" or "steam" position and allow all the steam to escape before opening the lid. Depending on what you're cooking, this can take from 1 to 5 minutes.

Natural Pressure Release, or "NPR": This is when you allow your pressure cooker to release built-up pressure naturally. When the cooking time is complete, turn off your appliance and wait until the float pin drops and you can safely open the lid. This can take anywhere from 10 to 30 minutes.

Combination of Natural Pressure Release and Quick Pressure Release: The recipe will call for a natural release for a specific amount of time and then a quick release of the remaining pressure before opening the lid. Example: "When the cook time is finished, allow a 10-minute natural release, then move the handle to the venting position and release any remaining steam. When the float pin drops, unlock the lid and open it carefully."

Regardless of which method your recipe requires, always make sure the float pin has dropped before opening the lid, and always open the lid away from you so you aren't accidentally burned by any residual steam.

Because models and brands vary widely, we strongly recommend you take the time to read the instruction manual that comes with your pressure cooker. It's important to know how your specific model works.

The Hot Water Test

Now that you are familiar with the basic parts of a pressure cooker, how it works, the safety features, and the pressure release methods, it's time to do an initial hot water test. This test is important and will enable you to see how your pressure cooker works. You'll get to see how quickly it comes to pressure, stays at pressure, and then releases pressure. Think of it as a troubleshooting test run. Basically, we're boiling water. We don't know about you, but we would much rather test something with a pot of water than be cooking a full meal and discover there may be a problem. Better to lose a few cups of water than a whole pot of expensive ingredients, right? Doing this test also gives you an opportunity to get comfortable with locking the lid in place, setting your pressure cooker, and using pressure release methods. Ready?

1. *First, put the inner pot inside the housing unit. This is a good habit to get into so you don't accidentally pour water (or any other liquids/ ingredients) into the housing unit by mistake.*
2. *Measure 3 cups (705 ml) water and pour it into the inner pot.*

3. *Inspect the lid to make sure the sealing ring is properly in place, then close and lock the lid.*
4. *Check to make sure the pressure release valve is closed. This is another good habit to have. Checking the valve every time you close the lid of your pressure cooker will save you from waiting forever for your cooker to come to pressure only to discover the release valve was open and now dinner will take even longer. Yes, we've done this. Many times. It's no fun.*
5. *Select Manual and set the timer on the control panel to cook for 5 minutes at high pressure.*
6. *Watch your unit carefully so you can see how it works. Take notes if you wish. It will take from 5 to 10 minutes for your unit to come to pressure. You may be able to hear the water inside begin to boil. You'll also see wisps of steam coming from the float valve. This is normal. The steam is what makes the float valve rise and seal. As you get to know your unit, you'll know when the valve seals because you'll hear a click or you'll notice a distinct lack of noise because the steam is no longer coming out. The timer will start once your unit is at pressure. This doesn't happen immediately after the float valve seals, but will begin within 1 to 2 minutes.*
7. *When the cook time is over, your unit will beep to let you know it's done. Carefully turn the pressure release valve to the open or venting position (some brands call it the Steam position) and allow the steam to escape. Remember, the steam is very hot and can burn you, so keep your face, hands, and arms away from it. It's also important to note which direction the steam is escaping. You may want to turn your pot so the steam doesn't hit the underside of a cabinet or any wall decorations you may have in your kitchen. If opening the pressure release valve makes you uncomfortable, you can use a pot holder or the handle of a long wooden spoon to gently move it to the open position.*
8. *Once the pressure and steam are released, you'll hear the float pin drop. On some models you can clearly see it drop back into the recessed position. This means the lid is unlocked and you can now open it safely.*
9. *Carefully open the lid, tilting it away from you so any residual steam and condensation that has collected under the lid doesn't drip on you or on the counter (or splash onto bare feet. Ouch!). There will always be condensation under the lid after cooking with a pressure cooker. When you open the lid, position it so the water drips back into the pot, instead of going elsewhere.*
10. *The inner pot will be hot. Use silicone mitts, pot holders, or a kitchen towel to remove it from the housing unit. Measure the amount of water left in the pot. You should see very little difference from the 3 cups (705 ml) water you added in the beginning. You may have lost 1 tablespoon (15 ml) or so, but nothing much above that. In a pressure cooker there is very little liquid lost to evaporation.*
11. *At this point, if you have chosen a brand that has a Keep Warm setting, you'll see the timer may have begun to count up. Press Cancel or unplug your machine. Different brands/models will allow you to turn off the Keep Warm setting so that when the cook time is over, the pressure cooker simply turns itself off. Either way, be sure to unplug your appliance when you're finished.*

That's it! You have successfully done your water test and are ready to create delicious meals for your whole family.

Basic Equipment

Trivet: A trivet or steam rack often comes standard with many electric pressure cookers. This rack keeps food, bowls, and pans elevated off the bottom of the inner cooking pot. This is an essential tool in your pressure-cooking arsenal. We also suggest purchasing a long-legged trivet that will fit in your pressure cooker. This is useful for several of our pot-in-pot recipes, as it allows more food underneath while still keeping another pot balanced safely above.

Steamer Basket: Generally speaking, when we say "steamer basket," we are referring to a collapsible basket made of stainless steel with overlapping side leaves that can be expanded to fit inside most 6- or 8-quart (5.4 or 7.2 L) pressure cookers. It has a colander-type basket and has feet, so it can be used to hold vegetables or proteins over boiling water to steam them. The center post, which occasionally has a ring on the end of it, can be used to help lift the basket from the inner pot. The center post is also removable, which makes it perfect for steaming larger vegetables like whole artichokes or spaghetti squash. You can find steamer baskets made of silicone or smaller baskets that double as strainers and come with lift handles that also fit easily inside most 6-quart (5.4 L) or larger pressure cookers.

Instant-Read Thermometer: (We recommend Thermapen from ThermoWorks.) An instant-read thermometer helps you check to ensure larger cuts of meats have been cooked to a safe internal temperature. It is also beneficial in ensuring your yogurt (if your pressure cooker has that function) has reached the proper temperature.

A 7 x 3-Inch (18 x 7.6 cm) Springform Pan or Push Pan: This is great to use for cheesecakes and lasagna. The sides of a springform pan expand and then buckle closed. It has a detachable bottom, which makes removing cheesecakes simple and easy. A push pan (we like Fat Daddio's) also has a removable bottom, but the sides of the pan are solid, so removing things like lasagna is nearly effortless.

A 7 x 3-Inch (18 x 7.6 cm) Round Cake Pan: If you can afford only one additional pan, make it this one. It's useful for cakes, spinach dip, frittatas, meatloaf, and pot-in-pot rice. If necessary, this pan can also be used for lasagna, but you will have difficulty removing your food.

A 6-Cup (1440 g) Bundt Pan: This half-size Bundt pan (we love Nordic Ware) fits perfectly inside most 6-quart (5.4 L) electric pressure cookers. Use it for cakes or bread pudding!

Small 4-Ounce (112 g) Mason Jars: These are sometimes called quilted jelly jars and are perfect for making individual-size cheesecakes or desserts.

Flat Wooden Spatula or Turner: This utensil helps scrape any browned bits off the bottom of the pot when you sauté your food and easily breaks up clumps when cooking ground meat.

A 1½ -Quart (1.4 L) Round Ceramic Casserole Dish without Handles: This is a great dish to have. It can double as a rice dish for pot-in-pot meals. It will fit a batch of Spinach Artichoke Dip (page 22) perfectly and fits seamlessly inside a 6-quart (5.4 L) pressure cooker.

Additional Silicone Rings: You will need to replace your sealing ring (sealing gasket) at least once a year. Thankfully they are not expensive. Some people have different colored gaskets that they switch out regularly for use when making sweet dishes versus savory dishes. The gaskets do tend to pick up odors, and who wants a cheesecake that smells like spaghetti and meatballs?

Aluminum Foil Sling: One of the best tools you will use with your pressure cooker is an aluminum sling. It will help you lift pans in and out of the pressure cooker with ease. The great thing about an aluminum sling? It is not expensive and you can use it over and over again. I keep mine in the same drawer as my plastic storage bags and parchment paper. First, tear off a sheet of aluminum foil about 24 inches (61 cm) long and lay it out on the kitchen table. Fold it lengthwise evenly into thirds, much like you were folding a piece of paper to put in an envelope. Run your hands over the edges to flatten it. Center the pan you want to lift in the middle of your newly created sling. Fold the edges up around the pan and bring the ends together. Twist the ends together to create a handle. Now you can safely place pans inside your pressure cooker without spilling the contents and, more importantly, you can lift hot pans out of the pressure cooker without burning your fingers. Some people like to create two slings for extra support on each side of the baking dish.

Silicone Pinch Mitts: Small, heat-resistant oven mitts designed to protect your hands and fingers from the hot inner cooking pot, these mitts allow you to grip the edges of the pot without getting burned. Most come with a textured grip surface to reduce the risk of slipping.

Retriever Tongs: These are different than traditional kitchen tongs. Retriever tongs are great for taking a very hot dish out of a container. They are designed to clip and lift the inner pot or steamer basket from your pressure cooker. They are also useful for taking hot plates from the oven or microwave without having to touch them.

Jar Lifter Tongs: This is a tool used often in canning. It is essential for lifting hot jars out of a water bath canner. It is also very useful for getting individual jars of cheesecake out of your pressure cooker.

Special Equipment and Accessories

Immersion Blender: This is a powerful stick blender. It is lightweight with sharp blades, and you can use it to blend foods right in your pressure cooker. You can mash potatoes, blend sauces, process hummus, and more. It usually comes with a whisk attachment and some kind of bowl or beaker, which also makes blending sauce or pesto easy and convenient.

Kitchen Scale: We recommend the OXO Good Grips Food Scale with an 11-pound (5 kg) capacity. This is especially important for your gluten-free baking needs. This scale will allow you to measure in both U.S. and metric increments. It has a zero function, which allows you to tare the scale with a bowl or other container before measuring so you'll have accurately measured ingredients every time.

Tips for Using Your Pressure Cooker Successfully

Always read the instruction manual that comes with your pressure cooker. It may seem boring or unnecessary, but the manuals are written for a reason. It's critical to your success to know your pressure cooker's strengths and limitations.

Never use your electric pressure cooker on the stovetop. There is a difference between a stove-top pressure cooker and an electric pressure cooker. Electric pressure cookers are meant to be stand-alone counter appliances. We've heard of people accidently melting their electric pressure cooker because they put it on a stovetop and a burner was mistakenly turned on underneath. For the purposes of this book, we focus solely on countertop electric pressure cookers.

Be aware of recipes and timing. This is imperative to keep in mind when planning your meals. Cooking in a pressure cooker is fast, but it does take time to put together. Always read through the entire recipe, sometimes twice. There is nothing worse than starting a recipe only to realize you are missing an essential ingredient. Consider the time it takes to prep your ingredients, then the time it takes for your pressure cooker to come to pressure. The same way an oven must preheat, pressure cookers need time to heat up and begin to build steam and pressure to cook your food. Also factor the total recipe cooking time and any specific pressure release time into your planning. A "3-minute" recipe might actually take 20 to 25 minutes depending on the temperature of your ingredients and how much liquid is in your pressure cooker.

NOTE:

All the recipes in this book were tested at or near sea level.

Altitude can make a difference! Because pressure cookers are built on the principle of boiling water to create steam, it's important to know that water boils at lower temperatures at higher elevations. For pressure cookers, shorter cooking times at a higher elevation is generally not a problem, but for longer cooking times or specific foods like grains or beans, you may need to make adjustments. A good, basic rule to follow is to add 5 percent more cooking time for each 1,000 feet (305 m) after 3,000 feet (915 m) above sea level. So if you live at 4,000 feet (1,220 m), you would add 10 percent; at 5,000 feet (1,524 m), add 15 percent; and so on. If you aren't sure, always use a food thermometer to help determine the temperature of your food. If you need to make adjustments from there, then you can do so safely.

Always ensure you have enough liquid in the inner pot to bring it to pressure. The minimum amount of liquid will vary depending on the brand of electric pressure cooker. Generally speaking, this is at least 1 cup (235 ml) of liquid, but check your owner's manual and always use tested recipes. Some recipes may call for less liquid because the food you are cooking releases a lot of water during the cooking process.

Do not overfill your pressure cooker. Pressure cookers require space for steam to build pressure and cook properly. A basic guideline is no more than two-thirds full for most recipes and half full for foods such as beans and grains, as they tend to expand and foam during cooking. Overfilling a pot can also create hazards and clog your vent pipes and valves. If your vents and valves get dirty, you'll need to clean them so your cooker can properly come to pressure.

If you hear popping noises, don't worry. This is common. Popping noises happen when the heating unit goes from one temperature to another and can happen occasionally if the bottom of your inner pot is wet. Be sure to dry it completely before starting to cook.

Some steam coming from the release valve is normal. Small wisps of steam will happen as the unit is coming to pressure before the float valve seals. However, if large plumes of steam continue for more than 2 minutes, check the valve to make sure it is set to sealing, not venting. If that doesn't fix the problem, you may have food debris on the float pin that is blocking the valve from sealing. Simply clean it according to your manufacturer's instructions and try again.

Brown meats or vegetables first, then deglaze the pot for more flavor. Many recipes will ask you to add oil or butter to the inner cooking pot and then brown or sauté an ingredient. Add the food in small batches and evenly brown the food on all sides. Remove the food to a serving plate or bowl, then use water, stock, or whatever liquid is specified in the recipe to loosen up and remove those delicious, cooked-on food particles left on the bottom of the pan. This is a great flavor enhancer for your dishes.

Follow instructions for thickening sauces. Many recipes designed for pressure cookers call for thickening the sauces and gravies after cooking. This is because pressure cookers use liquid to create steam and that liquid needs to be thin. Adding flour is a common way to thicken that flavorful cooking liquid in your pressure cooker, but for those who are gluten free, that is not an option. Instead, we use alternative thickeners. A cornstarch slurry (a mixture of cornstarch and water), arrowroot powder, or tapioca starch are good options for use in a pressure cooker. If your recipe calls for white beans, you can also blend ¼ cup (60 g) beans with ¼ cup (60 ml) of the cooking liquid into a bean slurry and use it to thicken soups and stews. Simmering the sauces until they're reduced is another option.

In this book, we'll give you guides to help if you are new to a gluten-free diet or only cook occasionally, help with setting up your kitchen, recommendations for gluten-free ingredients, and information you can use in all your gluten-free baking and cooking. Everyone, regardless of diet, can be a part of the pressure cooker revolution!

So, whether you are new to pressure cooking, new to gluten-free living, or are already an expert and simply want new recipes, we've got you covered. Come on, let's get cooking!

A Gluten-Free Kitchen and Home

Can You Use the Same Pressure Cooker for Regular And Gluten-Free Cooking?

If you will be cooking both regular and gluten-free foods for your family, we recommend you have two machines with one that is dedicated for gluten-free cooking only.

To help you tell them apart, use colored sealing rings and decals to indicate which machine is designated for gluten-free cooking. The Instant Pot Lux version also comes in several colors to make it even easier—find them on the Instant Pot website, https://instantpot.com/portfolio_entries/lux-series.

Creating a Gluten-free Kitchen

If the entire family is going to be eating gluten free, the first thing you need to do is clean out your kitchen (don't forget the refrigerator) and get rid of your gluten-full foods. Then hit the grocery store and restock your kitchen.

If you are worried about how to shop for groceries, stay to the periphery of the store, where they stock the fresh produce, meats, and dairy. Focusing on those will give you the most options for foods that are naturally safe for your entire family. Rice and potatoes are good, filling options to accompany main courses.

Creating a Dual-use Kitchen

In the instance where you can have a dual-use kitchen, shared equipment needs to be washed thoroughly after every use. Just make sure you don't use the same sponges or cloths to wash the gluten-free pans and dishes. For those items that cannot be fully submerged in water, like electrical appliances (toaster, panini press, toaster oven, etc.), it is safer to buy a second one to avoid cross-contamination.

Designating a single area for storing all your gluten-free food and cooking items will make it much easier for you and your gluten-free family members to know where their food is. If you have little ones, putting a strip of brightly colored duct tape on their containers of food can help them know which ones are theirs. This will keep them safe if they are looking for snacks when you are not around to supervise.

Equipment that is porous has to be separated, including cutting boards, storage containers, and wooden utensils. Stores sell sets of colored plastic cutting boards that will help you designate a specific color to be used with all gluten-free preparations. Buy a second toaster in a bright color so you can see which one to use right away. You can set up a cute pitcher and keep your gluten-free-specific mixing spoons and spatulas there. Buy a second set of food storage containers with different color tops and keep them on their own shelf.

Special Ingredient Considerations

Thickeners

When we want to thicken a sauce, we naturally reach for all-purpose flour, but when you are gluten free this is no longer an option. Thankfully, we are lucky that alternative thickeners are easy to find and make wonderful substitutions.

Cornstarch (or Cornflour in the UK): Cornstarch is the most efficient gluten-free thickener and our top choice. If you cannot have corn (sometimes found in conjunction with gluten sensitivities), choose one of the other starches below. Cornstarch must be dissolved in water before adding to cooking liquids to avoid clumps. It must also be brought to a full boil to activate it and then simmered for a few minutes to cook off any raw flavor.

Tapioca Starch (also called Tapioca Flour): Tapioca thickens at a much lower temperature, so keep the liquid just below a boil and do not stir for a long time if using this starch. Tapioca starch/flour is often carried at higher-end grocery stores in the baking aisle. If you cannot find it, it is readily available online.

Potato starch (not potato flour): Potato starch is very different from potato flour and cannot be used in the same way (especially important in baking applications). It is often sold in the same area as other starches in the baking aisle. Potato starch thickens very quickly with little to no flavor, making it great for a last-minute addition to thicken sauces. Do not cook too long or it may break down.

Arrowroot: This is an option for those who cannot have potatoes, corn, or nightshades in their diet. Arrowroot comes from the root of the plant; it is ground exceptionally finely, giving you extremely smooth sauces. Use at the very end of cooking and take off the heat once the sauce is at your desired thickness.

Oats

Oats can be confusing. Some people swear they can eat them and others have a reaction to them. Oats are often grown beside gluten crops and processed on the same equipment, frequently causing cross-contamination issues. There are a few vendors that sell certified gluten-free oats, such as Bob's Red Mill. Always look for a gluten-free certification and if you have any questions, contact the manufacturer directly.

Sausage, Ham, and Some Turkey

Most commercial sausages contain fillers that commonly include gluten ingredients. If you have a reputable butcher, you can ask them about what they put in their house-made sausages. If you want to buy sausages at the grocery store, some readily available brands that have gluten-free versions are Aidells, Jones Dairy Farm, and Boar's Head (read the labels). Commercially produced hams and turkeys often have gluten ingredients in the brine and injected liquids. Likewise, be careful with presliced and packaged deli meats—many will contain gluten ingredients. Always read the packaging carefully, look for a gluten-free certification, and if you have any questions, contact the manufacturer.

Soy Sauce

In the United States and elsewhere in the world, wheat is added to soy sauce (and other products made with it). It is used as a flavor enhancer and found in many foods. Tamari is another form of soy sauce and often is gluten free, but it is not guaranteed without certification. Look for gluten-free brands, clearly marked on the front label. You can substitute gluten-free soy sauce for regular in any recipe. If you cannot have soy, try coconut aminos, an excellent soy-free replacement.

Distilled Spirits

This is one of the most debated subjects in the gluten-free world. You will hear people strongly arguing on either side of the issue. The process of distillation destroys gluten, resulting in products that fall below the industry standard of 20 ppm. However, there are some people who may still react even below the standard. Another culprit may be because some distillers add caramel coloring to their alcohols, and these colorings often contain gluten ingredients. If you are cooking for someone with celiac or who is highly reactive, it is safer to use a grain-free alcohol like potato vodka for flavoring. Adding a teaspoon of brown sugar will make it a decent substitute for grain alcohol.

Wine

Wine is considered gluten free, but there may be a couple of gotchas for the most sensitive folks. Because it comes from grapes and not grain, it tests to well below the standard of 20 ppm. But there may be issues with added coloring or flavoring—usually found in dessert wines or wine coolers—so it pays to avoid those.

There are two primary sources of contamination in the wine industry: the caulking agents used with wooden aging barrels and the fining agents used to clarify wines. Some wooden barrels are sealed with a wheat-based caulk. Even though the chances of a reaction are slim, if you are having issues, look for winemakers who use stainless steel tanks. A less likely cause of a reaction could be the fining agents, particles winemakers use to make wines crystal clear. Reactions because of fining agents are rare, but if you are one of the few, you can contact the winery and ask what they use to clarify their wines.

In cooking, wine is often used to add flavor and interest to recipes. If you are hosting guests, feel free to ask them about their level of sensitivity and, in this case, whether they drink wine. If you are unsure how reactive your family or guests may be, you can always use stock or water and leave out the wine.

Our Recommended Flour Blend and Other Gluten-Free Flour Blends

When you are baking or cooking certain recipes, you will need to use a gluten-free all-purpose flour. If you will be baking a lot, making your own blend in bulk will save you money. If you are only using it occasionally, feel free to use a store-bought brand. Some of our favorites are Bob's Red Mill Gluten Free 1-to-1 Baking Flour, Pamela's All-Purpose Gluten-Free Flour, King Arthur Gluten-Free All-Purpose Flour, Cup4Cup Gluten-Free Flour Blend, and Authentic Foods' Gluten-Free Classical Blend.

In addition to gluten-free flours, a blend needs starches to give structure and lift to your baked goods. Starches are nearly always included, but it is not a given that the blend you buy includes gums or psyllium husk powder. Gums help hold your baked goods together and keep them from crumbling. If your commercial blend includes xanthan gum (or guar gum), reduce the amount called for in recipes by half. If you are sensitive to gums, you can use psyllium husk powder for the same purpose. Just use double the amount. So if the recipe calls for 1 teaspoon xanthan gum, replace that with 2 teaspoons psyllium husk powder.

To make it easier for you, we have included our favorite all-purpose blend to use in any baking and cooking recipes, both from this book and from other sources.

All-Purpose Gluten-Free Flour Blend

When you are baking or making recipes that call for flour, having a gluten-free blend already made and available is helpful. Use 120 grams of the blend for every 1 cup of flour called for in any recipe. This blend does not contain any dairy, nuts, or gums, making it very versatile. You can use it in everything calling for flour.

280 g (9.9 ounces, or 2¼ cups) sweet rice flour (not white rice flour)

280 g (9.9 ounces, or 2 ¼ cups) brown or white rice flour

120 g (4.2 ounces, or 1 cup plus 4¾ teaspoons) tapioca flour/starch

120 g (4.2 ounces, or ¾ cup) potato starch (not potato flour)

—

1.8 pounds, or about 6 cups (800 g)

Whisk the ingredients together and store in a large food-safe plastic bin. Secure the lid on the container and shake vigorously to distribute all the ingredients evenly.

Gluten-free flours tend to settle and sometimes separate while sitting, so always shake the container well before measuring for each baking project.

Appealing Appetizers

Recipes

Cherry Chipotle Chicken Wings (page 20)

Cherry Chipotle Chicken Wings

GLUTEN FREE • DAIRY FREE • NUT FREE • SOY FREE • PALEO

¼ cup (56 g) butter

1 cup (240 g) Not Ketchup Cherry Chipotle Sauce (or your favorite gluten-free BBQ/hot wing sauce)

1 tablespoon (15 ml) vegetable oil

3 to 4 pounds (1362 to 1816 g) chicken wings

Salt and pepper to taste

1 cup (235 ml) chicken stock

Gluten-free ranch dressing, for serving

Carrot and celery sticks, for serving

—

6 servings

NOTE:

You can buy Not Ketchup sauces online in a variety of different flavors, including a Spiced Fig and a Tangerine Hatch Chile that would also work well with this recipe. Check out their regular Fruitchup, Smoky Date, and Blueberry White Pepper, too! They are all gluten free, dairy free, and soy free!

In a small saucepan, melt the butter over low heat, then add the chipotle sauce. Cook over low heat, whisking continuously to combine. Simmer gently for 6 to 8 minutes, or until the sauce begins to thicken. Set aside.

Press Sauté on your electric pressure cooker. When the inner pot is hot, add the oil. Place the chicken wings in the pot and season with salt and pepper. Brown them for 5 minutes on each side. Remove to a serving plate.

Pour the chicken stock into the inner pot. Use a wooden spoon to gently scrape up any browned bits from the bottom of the pan.

Place a trivet in the bottom of the cooking pot over the stock. Place the browned wings on the trivet, being careful not to let the wings touch the stock.

Close and lock the lid, making sure the steam release knob is in the sealing position. Cook on high pressure for 5 minutes. When the cook time is finished, allow a 5-minute natural release, then do a quick release to vent any remaining steam. When the float pin drops, unlock the lid and open it carefully.

Line a baking sheet with aluminum foil. Remove the chicken wings from the pressure cooker and place on the lined baking sheet. If you have a rack that fits in the baking sheet, even better! The air circulating around the wings as they sit on the rack will make your wings extra crispy. If you don't have a rack, just put the wings on the foil-lined baking sheet. They will still get crispy.

Generously brush the wings with the warm sauce and broil for 7 minutes on each side. If they are not crispy enough, broil for 2 to 3 minutes more on each side.

Remove from the oven and, if desired, toss the wings quickly in the remaining sauce. Serve with gluten-free ranch dressing alongside some carrot and celery sticks.

Hummus

GLUTEN FREE • DAIRY FREE • VEGETARIAN

1 cup (240 g) dried chickpeas

3 cups (705 ml) water

1 teaspoon salt

3 tablespoons (45 ml) olive oil, plus more for serving

¼ cup (60 g) tahini

3 tablespoons (45 ml) lemon juice

4 cloves garlic, chopped roughly

1 teaspoon ground cumin

Salt and pepper to taste

Smoked paprika, for serving

Chopped fresh parsley, for serving

—

2 cups (480 g)

Add the dried chickpeas to the inner pot of your electric pressure cooker. Add the water and salt.

Close and lock the lid, making sure the steam release knob is in the sealing position. Cook on high pressure for 60 minutes. When the cook time is finished, allow a complete natural release. When the float pin drops, unlock the lid and open it carefully.

Ladle 1 cup (235 ml) of the cooking liquid out of the pot and set it aside. Using mitts or a dish towel, carefully lift the inner pot out and drain the chickpeas into a colander.

Transfer the warm, drained chickpeas to a food processor or blender. Add the olive oil, tahini, lemon juice, garlic, cumin, and salt. Process at medium speed, slowly adding in the reserved cooking liquid. Continue until the mixture is smooth and creamy. If needed, stop and scrape down the sides of the bowl and process again to achieve the desired texture. You might not use all of the cooking liquid.

Taste the hummus. Adjust the seasoning with salt and pepper, if needed.

Serve with a drizzle of olive oil and a sprinkle of smoked paprika and parsley. Store in an air-tight container for up to 6 days.

Spinach Artichoke Dip

GLUTEN FREE • SOY FREE • NUT FREE • VEGETARIAN

- 1 (10-ounce, or 280 g) package frozen spinach, thawed, chopped, and well drained
- 1 (14-ounce, or 392 g) can artichoke hearts, drained and coarsely chopped
- 4 cloves garlic, minced
- ½ cup (80 g) finely chopped onion
- 1 (8-ounce, or 227 g) block cream cheese, softened to room temperature and cut into cubes
- 1 cup (100 g) grated Parmesan cheese
- 1 cup (120 g) shredded mozzarella cheese
- ½ cup (120 g) sour cream or plain Greek yogurt
- ½ teaspoon salt
- ¾ teaspoon freshly ground black pepper
- ⅛ teaspoon cayenne pepper
- 2 cups (470 ml) water for the bottom of the pot
- Gluten-free crackers, for serving

—

10 servings

In a large bowl, or the bowl of your stand mixer, combine the spinach, artichokes, garlic, onion, cream cheese, Parmesan, mozzarella, sour cream, and seasonings. Mix well until thoroughly incorporated.

Spoon the mixture into a lightly greased 1½ quart (1.4 L) baking dish or a 7 x 3-inch (18 x 7.6 cm) cake pan that will fit in your pressure cooker. Cover the baking dish tightly with foil.

Place a trivet at the bottom of the inner pot of your pressure cooker and add the 2 cups (470 ml) water.

Using a foil sling (see page 11), carefully lower the casserole dish into the pressure cooker. Fold the foil strips down so that they do not interfere with closing the lid.

Close and lock the lid, making sure the steam release knob is in the sealing position. Cook on high pressure for 10 minutes. When the cook time is finished, use a quick release by opening the release knob and venting all the steam. When the float pin drops, unlock the lid and open it carefully.

Remove the foil-covered dish with the sling and check the dip to make sure the cheese is completely melted. Stir to combine. If you like a crispy top, slide the casserole dish under the broiler for 2 minutes until the cheese is a golden brown color. Watch carefully so it doesn't burn.

Serve warm with gluten-free crackers.

Delightfully Delicious Deviled Eggs

GLUTEN FREE • DAIRY FREE • SOY FREE • NUT FREE • VEGETARIAN • PALEO

FOR THE HARD-BOILED EGGS

1 cup (235 ml) cold water

12 large eggs, straight from the refrigerator

Large bowl of water with ice

FOR THE DEVILED EGGS

12 hard-boiled eggs

⅔ cup (160 g) mayonnaise

1 tablespoon (6 g) dry mustard powder

2 teaspoons (10 ml) hot sauce

Salt and pepper to taste

Smoked paprika, for garnish

Scallions, sliced on the diagonal, green parts only, for garnish

—

24 servings

HARD-BOILED EGGS: Pour the cold water in the inner cooking pot. Place a steam rack or trivet in the inner pot of your pressure cooker. Place the eggs on the trivet.

Close and lock the lid, making sure the steam release knob is in the sealing position. Cook on high pressure for 6 minutes (depending on how soft or firm you like the yolk). Naturally release the pressure for 6 minutes, then unlock the lid and open it carefully. Turn off the machine.

Remove the eggs and immediately plunge them into the bowl of ice water to stop the cooking. Let them sit for 6 to 10 minutes. If serving immediately, peel the eggs under running water. Store unpeeled eggs in the refrigerator up to 1 week.

DEVILED EGGS: Peel the hard-boiled eggs and slice in half. Remove the yolks and set aside.

In the bowl of a food processor, pulse hard egg yolks until they resemble yellow sand. Add the mayonnaise, mustard, and hot sauce. Blend until the mixture is smooth and creamy. If you don't have a food processor, combine the ingredients in a medium bowl and use a hand mixer to get the desired consistency. Add salt and pepper to taste.

Fill the hollows of the egg whites with the yolk mix. Sprinkle with smoked paprika and scallions to garnish.

Eggplant and Olive Spread

GLUTEN FREE • VEGETARIAN • DAIRY FREE

2 tablespoons (30 ml) olive oil

1 small brown onion, peeled and cut in half

2 pounds (908 g) eggplant, peeled and cut into large chunks

5 cloves garlic

1 tablespoon (4 g) fresh oregano leaves

1 teaspoon salt

1 cup (235 ml) vegetable stock

3 tablespoons (30 ml) lemon juice

1½ tablespoons (23 g) tahini

Salt and pepper, to taste

½ cup (50 g) pitted black olives (reserve a few for garnish)

1 tablespoon (2 g) chiffonade fresh Thai basil leaves, for garnish

¼ cup (40 g) diced cherry tomatoes, for garnish

Extra virgin olive oil, for drizzling

Gluten-free crackers or celery sticks, for serving

—

6 servings

NOTE:

Add a teaspoon of chili powder to the recipe if you like your dip on the spicy side.

Press Sauté on your electric pressure cooker. Adjust, if possible, to the highest setting. When the inner pot is hot, add the olive oil. When the oil has heated, carefully place the onion halves, cut side down, in the pot. Let them sear until the onions get very brown. Add the eggplant and garlic cloves. Let them get browned as well, watching carefully so the garlic cloves don't burn. Press Cancel.

Add the oregano, salt, and vegetable stock to the browned vegetables, stirring well.

Close and lock the lid, making sure the steam release handle is in the sealing position. Press Manual and cook on high pressure for 3 minutes. When the cook time is finished, do a quick pressure release by carefully moving the sealing handle to venting and allowing all the steam to escape. When the float pin drops, unlock the lid and open the lid carefully.

Using mini mitts or a dish towel, carefully remove the inner cooking pot from the base and strain the eggplant mixture in a large colander, reserving ¼ cup (60 ml) of the cooking liquid.

Place the eggplant mixture in a blender. Add the lemon juice, tahini, and olives. Blend, using some of the cooking liquid to help reach the desired consistency. You may not need all the liquid. Taste and adjust the seasoning, adding salt and pepper if needed.

Scrape into a serving bowl and sprinkle with the remaining whole olives, basil leaves, and tomatoes, and drizzle with the extra virgin olive oil. Serve with gluten-free crackers or celery sticks.

Nachos with Spicy Cheese Sauce

GLUTEN FREE • SOY FREE • NUT FREE

1 tablespoon (15 ml) vegetable oil

½ yellow onion, diced

2 poblano peppers, seeded and diced

2 teaspoons (6 g) chili powder

½ teaspoon ground cumin

½ teaspoon salt

1 (12-ounce, or 336 ml) bottle Ipswich Ale Brewery Celia Saison (or your favorite gluten-free beer)

1 (10-ounce, or 280 g) can diced tomatoes with jalapeños

12 ounces (336 g) sharp cheddar cheese, grated

12 ounces (336 g) Monterey Jack cheese, grated

3 tablespoons (24 g) cornstarch

Gluten-free corn tortilla chips, such as Mission brand, for serving (see Note)

Nacho toppings, as desired

—

8 servings

NOTE:

Be sure to use certified gluten-free tortilla chips. Some have wheat added and some are made in facilities where gluten-full products are also processed, posing a cross-contamination issue. It is always better to be careful and safe when serving those who cannot have gluten.

Press Sauté on your electric pressure cooker. When the inner pot is hot, add the oil. When the oil is hot, add the onion and poblano. Cook for 3 to 5 minutes, or until softened.

Add the chili powder, cumin, and salt and cook for 1 minute, or until very fragrant. Add the beer and diced tomatoes, scraping the bottom of the pan and stirring well to combine.

Close and lock the lid, making sure the steam release handle is in the sealing position. Cook on high pressure for 5 minutes.

While the sauce is cooking, in a bowl, toss the grated cheeses with the cornstarch, mixing well to make sure each shred is coated with the cornstarch.

When the cook time is finished, allow a 5-minute natural release, then do a quick release to vent any remaining steam. When the float pin drops, unlock the lid and open it carefully. Press Cancel.

Working quickly, add the coated cheese in handfuls to the beer mixture, whisking vigorously to combine. Once all of the cheese has been incorporated, set your pressure cooker to Keep Warm (if it has one) while you prepare the rest of the nachos. You may need to stir the sauce again before serving.

Scatter the tortilla chips on a platter, add your favorite nacho toppings, ladle the cheese sauce over the top, and enjoy!

Teriyaki Meatballs

GLUTEN FREE • NUT FREE

FOR THE TERIYAKI SAUCE

1 cup (235 ml) coconut aminos or gluten-free soy sauce

½ cup (120 ml) rice wine vinegar

4 cloves garlic, minced

1 tablespoon (8 g) freshly grated ginger

2 tablespoons (30 ml) vegetable oil

2 teaspoons (10 ml) sesame oil

⅓ cup (75 g) brown sugar

2 tablespoons (40 g) honey

1 teaspoon black pepper

FOR THE MEATBALLS

2 pounds (908 g) ground turkey meat (Jennie-O is gluten free)

½ cup (60 g) gluten-free panko bread crumbs

2 large eggs

½ cup (50 g) thinly sliced scallion, green parts only, divided

1 teaspoon garlic powder

1 teaspoon salt

1½ teaspoons freshly cracked black pepper

2 tablespoons (30 ml) vegetable oil

2 tablespoons (16 g) cornstarch

2 tablespoons (30 ml) cold water

1 tablespoon (8 g) sesame seeds, for garnish

—

40 meatballs

TERIYAKI SAUCE: Combine the coconut aminos, vinegar, garlic, ginger, vegetable oil, sesame oil, brown sugar, honey, and pepper in a medium bowl. Set aside.

MEATBALLS: In a large bowl, combine the ground turkey, bread crumbs, eggs, ¼ cup (25 g) of the scallions, garlic powder, salt, and pepper. Using a scant 1 ounce (28 g), gently shape into 40 meatballs.

Press Sauté on your electric pressure cooker. When the inner pot is hot, add the oil. When the oil is hot, add enough meatballs to cover the bottom of the pot, browning for about 2 minutes per side. Remove to a serving platter while you brown the rest.

When all the meatballs are browned, return them to the pot and pour the teriyaki sauce over them.

Close and lock the lid, making sure the steam release handle is in the sealing position. Cook on high pressure for 15 minutes. When the cook time is finished, allow a natural release for 10 minutes, then do a quick release to vent any remaining steam. Once the float pin drops, you can safely unlock the lid. Press Cancel.

In a small bowl, whisk together the cornstarch and water until it forms a slurry. Press Sauté and when the mixture starts to bubble, add the slurry to the pot, continuing to stir until the sauce thickens considerably around the meatballs, 3 to 5 minutes.

To serve, transfer the meatballs to a large platter. Skewer each one with a decorative toothpick and sprinkle with the remaining ¼ cup (25 g) sliced scallions and the sesame seeds.

Spectacular Soups and Stews

Recipes

Black Bean Soup with Cilantro-Lime Cream *(page 38)*

Dreamy Creamy Tomato Soup

GLUTEN FREE • VEGETARIAN • SOY FREE • NUT FREE • EGG FREE

2 tablespoons (28 g) butter or (30 ml) olive oil, divided

1 medium onion, finely chopped

3 carrots, finely chopped

3 stalks celery, finely chopped

½ red bell pepper, seeded and finely chopped

1 clove garlic, minced

2 cups (470 ml) chicken stock

About 50 ounces (1,500 g) chopped or crushed tomatoes, such as Pomi brand

2 teaspoons (1 g) dried oregano

2 teaspoons (1 g) dried basil

½ teaspoon dried crushed rosemary

1 bay leaf

1 teaspoon granulated sugar

2 teaspoons (12 g) kosher or fine sea salt

1 teaspoon freshly ground black pepper

½ cup (120 ml) heavy cream or half-and-half

2 tablespoons (4 g) finely minced fresh basil leaves, plus whole leaves for garnish

—

About 4 servings

Press Sauté and heat the inner pot of your electric pressure cooker. Melt 1 tablespoon (14 g) of the butter. Add the onion, carrots, celery, and bell pepper and cook for 3 minutes, stirring, to soften. Stir in the garlic and cook for 30 seconds. Add the stock, tomatoes, herbs, sugar, salt, and pepper. Stir to combine. Press Cancel.

Close and lock the lid, making sure the steam release handle is in the sealing position. Cook on high pressure for 5 minutes. When it is finished, release the pressure naturally for 10 minutes, then turn the steam release handle to venting, releasing any remaining steam. Unlock the lid and open it carefully. Press Cancel.

Remove and discard the bay leaf. Stir in the remaining 1 tablespoon (14 g) butter and stir until it is melted. Use an immersion blender to puree the soup in the pot. You can also use a blender, but puree in batches—hot liquids expand!

Stir in the cream and chopped basil. Taste and adjust the seasonings if needed. Ladle into bowls, garnish with basil leaves, and serve.

NOTE:

When a recipe highlights an ingredient like this recipe does tomatoes, it pays to use the best you can afford. Pomi brand tomatoes are imported from Northern Italy and are consistently high quality for the best-tasting recipes. They come in boxes and can be found at many major grocery stores across the nation.

Vegan Wild Rice Soup with Cashew Cream

GLUTEN FREE • DAIRY FREE • VEGETARIAN • VEGAN • SOY FREE • EGG FREE

FOR THE SOUP

2 tablespoons (30 ml) olive or vegetable oil

1½ cups (240 g) diced onion

3 cloves garlic, minced

1 cup (130 g) diced carrot

1 cup (120 g) diced celery

1 cup (230 g) organic dried chickpeas, soaked for 4 hours or overnight and drained

1¼ cups (200 g) organic wild rice or a wild rice blend

1 bay leaf

1 tablespoon (2 g) fresh thyme leaves

5 cups (1,175 ml) vegetable stock or water

Kosher or fine sea salt and freshly ground black pepper, to taste

FOR THE CASHEW CREAM (OPTIONAL)

½ cup (55 g) raw cashews, soaked for 30 minutes in hot water and then drained

½ cup (120 ml) fresh water

—

About 6 servings

NOTE:

Using homemade vegetable stock lets you control the flavor profile and the quality of the ingredients. This soup is perfect for lunch or as the starter for a bigger meal.

SOUP: Press Sauté on your electric pressure cooker. Add the oil to the inner pot and when it is hot, add the onions. Cook the onions until softened and translucent, about 4 minutes. Add the garlic and cook for 30 seconds, until fragrant. Stir in the carrots and celery. Cook until the vegetables are softened, about 4 minutes.

Add the drained chickpeas, wild rice, bay leaf, thyme, and stock. Stir well. Close and lock the lid, making sure the steam release handle is in the sealing position. Cook on high pressure for 25 minutes.

CASHEW CREAM: While the soup is cooking, make the cashew cream. Blend the soaked and drained cashews with the ½ cup (120 ml) fresh water in a blender until completely smooth. Set aside.

When the soup is finished, release the pressure naturally. Turn the steam release handle to venting, releasing any remaining steam. When the float pin drops, unlock the lid and open it carefully. Stir in the cashew cream (if using) until completely incorporated. Add salt and pepper to taste. Serve immediately.

Beef "Barley" Soup with Sorghum

GLUTEN FREE • DAIRY FREE • SOY FREE • NUT FREE

2 tablespoons (30 ml) olive or vegetable oil

1½ pounds (680 g) beef chuck roast, fat trimmed and meat cut into 1-inch (2.5 cm) cubes

1 large onion, chopped

2 cloves garlic, minced

2 carrots, trimmed and chopped

2 stalks celery, trimmed and chopped

1 tablespoon (15 g) tomato paste

1 teaspoon minced fresh rosemary leaves

1 teaspoon fresh thyme leaves

6½ cups (1,528 ml) beef stock or gluten-free store-bought stock (see Note)

1 cup (200 g) whole-grain sorghum, rinsed and drained

2 bay leaves

Kosher or fine sea salt and ground black pepper, to taste

—

About 4 servings

Press Sauté and pour the oil into the inner pot of your electric pressure cooker. Brown the beef on all sides, working in batches so you can leave room between the pieces as they cook. Transfer the browned beef to a plate; set aside.

Add the onion and garlic to the oil in the pot. Cook, stirring often, until the onion has begun to soften, about 3 minutes. Stir in the carrots, celery, tomato paste, rosemary, and thyme. Cook for another 3 minutes, stirring regularly. Pour in the stock and scrape the bottom of the pot to release any browned bits. Add the sorghum and bay leaves. Return the beef to the pot. Press Cancel.

Close and lock the lid, making sure the steam release handle is in the sealing position. Cook on high pressure for 40 minutes. When it is finished, release the pressure naturally for 10 minutes, then turn the steam release handle to venting, releasing remaining steam. Unlock the lid and carefully open.

Taste the stock and adjust the seasoning with salt and pepper as desired. Remove and discard the bay leaves. Ladle into bowls and serve.

NOTES:

Whole-grain sorghum can be challenging to find. If it isn't readily available in your local grocery store, you can order it online from Bob's Red Mill (www.bobsredmill.com).

Using homemade stock lets you control the amount of salt in your dishes. If you use canned beef stock, it will likely be saltier than homemade. If you taste the soup and it is too salty, you can add more water to dilute it.

Spicy Butternut Squash Soup

GLUTEN FREE • DAIRY FREE • VEGETARIAN • VEGAN • SOY FREE • NUT FREE • EGG FREE

1 large butternut squash

3 tablespoons (45 ml) olive or vegetable oil, divided

2 large shallots, minced

3 stalks celery, trimmed and finely chopped

2 carrots, trimmed and finely chopped

2 teaspoons (2 g) fresh thyme leaves

2 cloves garlic, minced

3 cups (705 ml) vegetable stock or gluten-free store-bought stock, divided (see Note, page 32)

2 tablespoons (30 ml) maple syrup or agave syrup, or to taste

1 teaspoon kosher or fine sea salt

½ teaspoon freshly ground black pepper

¼ teaspoon hot sauce, or to taste (Sriracha brand is gluten free)

Chopped chives, for garnish

—

4 to 6 servings

Place the squash in the microwave and heat for 1 to 2 minutes. This softens the rind and makes it easier and safer to cut. Using a large, sharp knife, cut the squash into quarters, scrape out the seeds and strings, and peel the chunks. Cut into cubes.

Press Sauté and add the oil to the inner pot. When it is hot, add the shallots, celery, carrots, and thyme and cook 4 minutes, stirring often, or until softened. Add the garlic and cook for 30 seconds. Add 1 cup (235 ml) of the stock to the pot, scraping the bottom to release any browned bits. Add the remaining 2 cups (470 ml) stock, maple syrup, salt, pepper, hot sauce, and butternut squash. Press Cancel.

Close and lock the lid, making sure the steam release handle is in the sealing position. Cook on high pressure for 9 minutes. When it is finished, release the pressure naturally for 10 minutes, then release the remaining pressure by turning the steam release handle to venting. When the pressure valve drops, unlock the lid and open it carefully. Check to make sure the squash is fork-tender. If it needs more time, replace the lid, return to pressure, and cook for another 2 or 3 minutes.

Use an immersion blender to puree the soup right in the inner pot, or transfer half of the soup at a time to a blender and puree in batches. Taste the soup and adjust the seasonings as needed. If the soup is too thick, add a little more stock or water. Ladle into serving bowls, sprinkle with the chives, and serve hot.

NOTE:

To make this even easier and save you time, you can buy the squash already cleaned and cubed at many grocery stores. This takes care of the bulk of the chopping and lets you relax and let the pressure cooker do all the work!

Pasta e Fagioli (Italian Bean and Pasta Soup)

GLUTEN FREE • DAIRY-FREE OPTION • VEGETARIAN OPTION • SOY FREE • NUT FREE • EGG FREE

FOR THE PASTA

6 ounces (168 g) elbow pasta, such as Barilla gluten-free brand

2 teaspoons (12 g) kosher or fine sea salt

Olive or vegetable oil

FOR THE SOUP

2 tablespoons (30 ml) olive oil

1 medium onion, finely chopped

1 carrot, finely chopped

1 stalk celery, finely chopped

1 pound (454 g) gluten-free ground turkey or ground pork

1 teaspoon thyme leaves

1 teaspoon dried oregano

1 teaspoon chili powder (McCormick and Penzeys brands have gluten-free versions)

½ teaspoon dried ground rosemary

½ teaspoon kosher or fine sea salt

¼ teaspoon freshly ground black pepper

3 cloves garlic, chopped

¼ cup (60 ml) gluten-free dry white wine or water (see Note, page 51)

2 cups (470 g) tomato sauce or crushed tomatoes

1 quart (940 ml) chicken stock or vegetable stock

2 bay leaves

1 (15-ounce, or 420 g) can gluten-free cannellini beans, rinsed and drained

Grated Parmigiano-Reggiano or Romano cheese or your favorite dairy-free cheese, for serving

Roughly chopped fresh basil leaves, for serving

—

6 to 8 servings

PASTA: Place the pasta in the inner pot of your electric pressure cooker, cover with water, and sprinkle with the salt. Stir to make sure nothing is sticking to the bottom of the pot. Close and lock the lid, making sure the steam release handle is in the sealing position. Cook on high pressure for 1 minute, release the pressure naturally for 4 minutes, then do a controlled release by holding the handle halfway between the open and closed positions. Protect your hand with an oven hot pad. When all the steam has been released, press Cancel.

When the float pin drops, unlock the lid and open it carefully. Pour the pasta into a colander and drain. Rinse with cool water to stop the cooking. Drizzle with a little oil and toss to keep the pasta from sticking together as it sits. Set aside and stir occasionally.

(continued)

SOUP: Press Sauté and heat the oil in the inner pot of your electric pressure cooker. Add the onion, carrot, and celery, cooking until softened, about 4 minutes, stirring occasionally. Add the meat and cook until browned, using a flat spatula to break up clumps. Season with the thyme, oregano, chili powder, rosemary, salt, and pepper. When the meat is cooked through, stir in the garlic and cook for an additional 30 seconds, until fragrant. Pour in the wine and deglaze the pot, scraping up any browned bits off the bottom.

Stir in the tomato sauce and stock, then add the bay leaves and drained beans. Close and lock the lid, making sure the steam release handle is in the sealing position. Cook on high pressure for 3 minutes. When it is finished, release the pressure naturally for 10 minutes, then turn the steam release handle to venting, releasing any remaining steam. When the pressure valve drops, unlock the lid and open it carefully. Press Cancel.

Stir the cooked pasta into the pot, replace the lid, and let sit for a few minutes to reheat. Taste and adjust the seasonings if needed. Ladle the soup into bowls, top with some of the cheese and basil, and serve immediately.

NOTE:

The timing for the pasta may change depending on the brand of pasta you use. See page 56 for details.

Chile Verde Pork Stew

GLUTEN FREE • DAIRY FREE • SOY FREE • NUT FREE • EGG FREE

FOR THE HOMEMADE SALSA VERDE

2 pounds (908 g) fresh New Mexico or poblano chiles, seeded and chopped

1 pound (454 g) fresh tomatillos, husked and rinsed well, or 1 (28-ounce, or 784 g) can whole tomatillos

1 jalapeño pepper, seeded and chopped (optional)

¼ cup (4 g) fresh cilantro leaves

½ teaspoon onion powder (*not* onion salt)

Pinch each of kosher or fine sea salt and freshly ground black pepper

FOR THE CHILE VERDE

3 pounds (1362 g) pork shoulder or pork butt

2 tablespoons (30 ml) olive or vegetable oil, divided

2 cups (470 ml) chicken stock

1 onion, chopped

4 cloves garlic, minced

1 tablespoon (2 g) dried oregano

2 teaspoons (6 g) ground cumin

1 teaspoon chipotle powder (optional)

1½ cups (355 g) salsa verde, homemade (see below) or store-bought

Kosher or fine sea salt and freshly ground black pepper, to taste

STEAMED RICE FOR SERVING

Fresh lime wedges, for serving

Gluten-free corn tortillas, such as Mission brand, for serving (see Note)

—

6 to 8 servings

SALSA VERDE: Place the chiles and fresh husked tomatillos on a baking sheet. If using canned tomatillos, no need to cook them. Place the baking sheet under the broiler and cook for about 4 minutes, until the chiles are blistered and the tomatillos have brown spots on them. Turn everything over and broil again for about 3 minutes, or until blackened. Transfer the chiles to a bowl and cover with a clean kitchen towel. Let them steam for a few minutes. Peel the blackened skins off the chiles. Combine the chiles (with their juices), tomatillos, jalapeño, cilantro, and onion powder in a blender. Add a pinch of salt and blend until smooth. Pour into a measuring cup. Add enough water to bring this to 2 cups (470 ml) and stir to blend. Taste and adjust the seasonings if needed.

(continued)

NOTE:

Just because you find corn tortillas doesn't mean they are gluten-free. Many manufacturers add it because wheat flour helps keep them pliable, making them unsafe for anyone following a gluten-free diet. Always carefully read the labels of every product you buy!

CHILE VERDE: Trim the fat from the meat and cut into 1-inch (2.5 cm) cubes. Press Sauté on your electric pressure cooker. Heat 1 tablespoon (15 ml) of the oil until shimmering in the inner pot. Add the pork in batches, browning on all sides. Use a slotted spoon to transfer the pork to a plate and continue browning the rest of the pork. When the pork is browned, place all of it back in the inner pot and add the chicken stock. Be sure to scrape the bottom of the pot to release any browned bits. Close and lock the lid, making sure the steam release handle is in the sealing position. Cook on high pressure for 20 minutes.

When it is finished, release the pressure naturally for 10 minutes, and then quick release the remaining steam. Unlock the lid and open it carefully. Use a slotted spoon to transfer the pork to a bowl; set aside. Press Cancel. Strain the cooking liquid through a fat separator or skim the fat from the surface and keep the remaining liquid separately.

Add the remaining 1 tablespoon (15 ml) oil to the pot and press Sauté. When hot, add the onion and cook, stirring, until softened, about 3 minutes. Add the garlic, oregano, cumin, and chipotle (if using) and cook just until fragrant, about 30 seconds. Add the cooked pork and stir everything together to distribute the seasonings. Pour in the salsa verde plus as much of the reserved cooking liquid as you need to reach the consistency you like. Cook for 3 minutes to blend the flavors. Taste and adjust the seasonings if needed.

Serve hot over cooked rice with fresh lime wedges and gluten-free corn tortillas.

NOTE:

For a faster option, if you can find a gluten-free salsa verde in your area, you can substitute that for the homemade version, but homemade always tastes better!

Black Bean Soup with Cilantro-Lime Cream

GLUTEN FREE • DAIRY-FREE OPTION • VEGETARIAN • VEGAN OPTION • SOY FREE • NUT FREE • EGG FREE

FOR THE SOUP

16 ounces (454 g) dried black beans

2 tablespoons (30 ml) olive oil

1 large onion, finely chopped

1 large red bell pepper, cored, seeded, and finely chopped

2 stalks celery, trimmed and finely chopped

1 clove garlic, minced

1 tablespoon (3 g) dried oregano

1 tablespoon (6 g) ground cumin

1½ teaspoons kosher salt

½ teaspoon freshly ground black pepper

½ to 1 teaspoon chipotle powder, to taste

4 cups (940 ml) vegetable stock or water, divided

Juice of ½ to 1 fresh lime

FOR THE CILANTRO-LIME CREAM

(omit for dairy free and vegan)

¾ cup (180 g) sour cream

Juice of ½ to 1 fresh lime

¼ cup (4 g) fresh cilantro leaves, rinsed well and patted dry

½ to 1 teaspoon chipotle powder, to taste

Kosher or fine sea salt and ground white pepper, to taste

For optional garnishes

Chopped fresh cilantro leaves

Chopped scallion

Chopped ripe tomatoes

Fresh lime wedges

—

About 6 servings

NOTE:

If you forgot to soak the beans overnight, don't worry, you can still make the soup. Place the sorted beans in a sauce pot and add enough water to cover by 3 inches (7.6 cm). Bring to a boil and cook for 1 minute. Turn off the heat, cover, and let the beans rest for 1 hour. Drain and cook as directed above.

SOUP: Sort the beans, discarding any pebbles or debris, rinse them well, and drain. Place in a large bowl and cover with fresh water. Loosely cover and set aside overnight. Drain before adding to the soup. (See Note.)

Press Sauté on your electric pressure cooker. Add the oil to the inner pot and when hot, add the onion, bell pepper, and celery. Cook, stirring often, until the vegetables have softened, about 4 minutes. Add the garlic, oregano, cumin, salt, pepper, and chipotle powder. Stir to evenly coat all the vegetables with the seasonings. Add 1 cup (235 ml) of the stock, scraping the bottom of the pot to release any browned bits. Pour in the remaining 3 cups (705 ml) stock and the soaked and drained black beans; stir well. Press Cancel.

(continued)

Close and lock the lid, making sure the steam release handle is in the sealing position. Cook on high pressure for 12 minutes.

CILANTRO-LIME CREAM: While the soup is cooking, make the cream. Combine the sour cream, lime juice (start with juice of ½ lime), cilantro, and chipotle powder in a food processor. Run the motor until the herbs are completely pureed and smooth. Taste and add salt and pepper. Add more lime juice or cilantro if you want a bolder, brighter flavor, but remember that flavors intensify over time. Transfer to a bowl and set aside while the soup finishes cooking.

FINISH THE SOUP: When the soup is finished, release the pressure naturally for 10 minutes, then turn the steam release handle to venting, releasing any remaining steam. Unlock the lid and open it carefully.

Use an immersion blender to puree the soup or transfer to a blender and puree in batches. You can leave some of the beans whole for a chunkier texture or puree until completely smooth. Stir in the fresh lime juice. Taste and adjust the seasonings. Ladle into serving bowls, add a dollop of the cream (if using), and top with your desired garnishes. Serve immediately.

NOTE:

When you are working with dried beans, be very careful to check for small stones or bits of rock. It is common to find some in nearly every bag. Spread the beans out on a baking sheet with sides, which will contain them. Working in sections, sort through all of the beans, discarding any debris you find. Rinse the beans well and drain before continuing with the recipe.

Chile Tortilla Soup

GLUTEN FREE • DAIRY-FREE OPTION • VEGETARIAN OPTION • SOY FREE • NUT FREE • EGG FREE

FOR THE TORTILLA STRIPS

Gluten-free corn tortillas, such as Mission brand (see Note, page 36)

Olive oil, for brushing

Kosher salt and ancho chile powder

FOR THE SOUP

2 tablespoons (30 ml) olive or vegetable oil

1 medium onion, finely chopped

2 carrots, trimmed and finely chopped

2 stalks celery, trimmed and finely chopped

1 tablespoon (8 g) ancho chile powder or gluten-free chili powder (McCormick and Penzeys have many gluten-free offerings), or to taste

2 teaspoons (6 g) ground cumin

1 teaspoon dried oregano

1 clove garlic, minced

1 quart (940 ml) chicken stock, divided

16 ounces (454 g) crushed or strained tomatoes

2 to 2½ pounds (908 to 1,135 g) boneless, skinless chicken thighs

¼ cup (30 g) gluten-free masa harina or corn flour (Bob's Red Mill brand is gluten free)

2 cups (260 g) frozen corn kernels

FOR THE GARNISHES

Fresh cilantro leaves

Avocado chunks

Shredded cheese such as pepper Jack, cheddar, or Colby

—

4 to 6 servings

TORTILLA STRIPS: Preheat the oven to 350°F (180°C, or gas mark 4). Brush the tortillas on both sides with the oil and cut into thin strips. Spread them out on a parchment-lined baking sheet, sprinkle with salt and chile powder, and bake until lightly golden brown and slightly crispy, tossing occasionally; about 15 minutes. Remove from the oven and set aside.

SOUP: Press Sauté and heat the inner pot of your electric pressure cooker. Add the oil and, when hot, add the onions, carrots, and celery. Sprinkle with the chile powder, cumin, and oregano. Cook, stirring often, for about 4 minutes to slightly soften the vegetables. Stir in the garlic and cook for 30 seconds. Add 1 cup (235 ml) of the stock to deglaze the pan, scraping up any browned bits from the bottom of the pot. Pour in the remaining 3 cups (705 ml) stock and the tomatoes. Press Cancel.

Tuck the chicken into the liquids, then close and lock the lid, making sure the steam release handle is in the sealing position. Cook on high pressure for 12 minutes. When it is finished, release the pressure naturally for 15 minutes, then turn the steam release handle to venting, releasing any remaining steam. Press Cancel. Unlock the lid and open it carefully.

Transfer the chicken to a cutting board and chop or shred into small bite-size pieces. Press Sauté, whisk the masa harina into the soup, and bring to a boil, stirring constantly until thickened slightly. Return the chicken pieces to the pot and stir in the corn kernels. Press Cancel, place the lid on the pressure cooker, and leave to rest for 6 minutes to reheat the chicken and corn. Taste and adjust the seasonings if needed.

SERVE: Ladle the soup into bowls and garnish with the crispy tortilla strips, cilantro, and avocado. Sprinkle cheese on top and serve immediately.

Great Grains and Rice

Recipes

Millet and Chicken Greek Salad
(page 52)

Perfect Rice Every Time (White and Brown Varieties)

GLUTEN FREE • DAIRY FREE • VEGETARIAN • VEGAN • SOY FREE • NUT FREE • EGG FREE

FOR WHITE RICE

1 cup (180 g) long-grain white rice

1¼ cups (295 ml) water or vegetable stock

½ teaspoon kosher or fine sea salt, or to taste

FOR BROWN RICE

1 cup (190 g) brown rice

1½ cups (355 ml) water or vegetable stock

½ teaspoon kosher or fine sea salt, or to taste

—

3 to 4 servings

NOTE:

Although there is a "Rice" function on most of today's electric pressure cookers, they are mostly designed for white and converted rice. When cooking other types of rice, it is best to manually set the machine.

WHITE RICE: Place the rice in a fine-mesh strainer and rinse under cold water until the water runs clear, about 1 minute. In the inner pot of your electric pressure cooker, stir together the rice, water, and salt. Close and lock the lid, making sure the steam release handle is in the sealing position. Cook on high pressure for 3 minutes.

When it is finished, release the pressure naturally for 12 minutes, then turn the steam release handle to venting, releasing any remaining steam. Unlock the lid and open it carefully. Use a fork to rake and fluff the rice before serving.

BROWN RICE: Place the rice in a fine-mesh strainer and rinse under cold water until the water runs clear, about 1 minute. Stir together the rice, water, and salt in the inner pot of your electric pressure cooker. Close and lock the lid, making sure the steam release handle is in the sealing position. Cook on high pressure for 22 minutes.

When it is finished, release the pressure naturally for 10 minutes, then turn the steam release handle to venting, releasing any remaining steam. Unlock the lid and open it carefully. Use a fork to rake and fluff the rice before serving.

Savory Creamy Polenta

GLUTEN FREE • DAIRY-FREE OPTION • VEGETARIAN/VEGAN OPTION • SOY FREE • NUT FREE

1 cup (164 g) polenta or medium-grind cornmeal

4 cups (940 ml) water or vegetable stock

1 teaspoon kosher or fine sea salt

¼ cup (60 ml) heavy cream or half-and-half (optional)

½ cup (50 g) grated Parmesan cheese (optional)

—

About 4 servings

Place the polenta, water, and salt in the inner pot of your electric pressure cooker. Stir well. Close and lock the lid, and make sure the steam release handle is in the sealing position before cooking on high for 5 minutes. When it is finished, allow the pressure to release naturally for 12 minutes. Then turn the steam release handle to venting, releasing any remaining steam. Unlock the lid and open it carefully.

Stir well with a whisk until the mixture becomes creamy and smooth, making sure to break up lumps. If desired, stir in the cream for additional richness. Scoop into bowls, sprinkle with the cheese, if using, and serve.

NOTES:

For a sweet version, use water and no cheese. Top bowls of cooked polenta with brown sugar or maple syrup just before serving.

Polenta and other cornmeal preparations will stick to the cooking pot if it is not immediately rinsed. Never wait too long to fill the pot with soapy water or your cleanup will be much more challenging.

Quinoa Vegetable Salad with Lemon Vinaigrette

GLUTEN FREE • DAIRY FREE • VEGETARIAN • VEGAN • SOY FREE • NUT FREE • EGG FREE

FOR THE QUINOA

1 cup (235 ml) vegetable stock or water

¼ cup (60 ml) water

1 cup (175 g) quinoa, very well rinsed and drained

1 teaspoon kosher or fine sea salt

FOR THE LEMON VINAIGRETTE

2 tablespoons (30 ml) freshly squeezed lemon juice

¼ cup (60 ml) extra virgin olive oil

1 teaspoon honey (or to taste)

½ teaspoon fresh thyme leaves

¼ teaspoon kosher or fine sea salt

⅛ teaspoon freshly ground black pepper

FOR THE VEGETABLES

1 tablespoon (15 ml) olive or vegetable oil

2 large carrots, trimmed and finely chopped

2 stalks celery, trimmed and finely chopped

1 large red bell pepper, cored, seeded, and finely chopped

2 tablespoons (20 g) minced red onion

1 cup (150 g) cherry tomatoes, quartered

1 medium cucumber, peeled, seeded, and finely chopped

2 scallions, trimmed and thinly sliced

2 teaspoons (1 g) fresh thyme leaves

—

4 to 6 servings

QUINOA: Place the stock, water, quinoa, and salt in the inner pot of your electric pressure cooker. Stir and put the lid on the pot. Lock the lid, making sure the steam release handle is in the sealing position. Cook on high pressure for 4 minutes. When the quinoa is finished, let the pressure release naturally for 12 minutes, then turn the steam release handle to venting, releasing any remaining steam. Unlock the lid and open it carefully.

Transfer the quinoa to a bowl and set aside. Wipe out the pot and return to the pressure cooker.

VINAIGRETTE: While the quinoa is cooking, make the vinaigrette. In a bowl or jar with a tight lid, whisk together the dressing ingredients until emulsified. If using a jar, you can shake it vigorously to blend. Taste and adjust the seasonings as needed.

VEGETABLES: Press Sauté and heat the oil in the inner pot. Add the carrots, celery, bell pepper, and onion and cook, stirring often, until the onion is softened, about 3 minutes. Press Cancel.

Add the sautéed vegetables to the cooked quinoa. Stir in the tomatoes, cucumber, and scallion. Sprinkle the thyme over the top. Dress the salad with about 3 tablespoons (45 ml) of the vinaigrette, tossing to coat the grains and vegetables. Taste and adjust the seasonings, adding more vinaigrette if desired. Place the salad in the refrigerator and chill until ready to serve. The flavors will blend as it rests. Toss again before serving. Can be served cool or at room temperature.

Andouille and Chicken Jambalaya

GLUTEN FREE • DAIRY FREE • SOY FREE • NUT FREE • EGG FREE

1 tablespoon (15 ml) olive or vegetable oil

3 (1⅔ pounds, 815 g) boneless chicken breast halves, cut into ½-inch (1.3 cm) cubes

12 ounces (340 g) Cajun-style Andouille sausage, thinly sliced

1 large onion, finely diced

4 stalks celery, finely diced

2 green bell peppers, cored and finely diced

1½ cups (270 g) long-grain white rice, rinsed

2 bay leaves

2 teaspoons (1 g) dried thyme leaves

1 teaspoon dried oregano

1 teaspoon smoked paprika

½ teaspoon chipotle powder

1 teaspoon salt

½ teaspoon freshly ground black pepper

3 cloves garlic, minced

1½ cups (355 ml) chicken stock or vegetable stock

1 (14-ounce, or 392 g) can gluten- free crushed tomatoes

Chopped fresh parsley, for garnish

—

6 to 8 servings

Press Sauté. When the inner pot is hot, pour in the oil. Add the chicken and cook for about 4 minutes, until partially cooked. Add the sausage, stirring often, for another 5 minutes, or until the chicken is cooked through. Transfer the meats to a bowl. Set aside.

Stir the onions, celery, and bell peppers into the inner pot. Cook until the vegetables have softened, about 8 minutes, stirring often. Add the rice and seasonings, stirring to coat the rice with the oil, then stir in the garlic. Cook for 30 seconds, stirring, until the garlic is fragrant. Press Cancel.

Pour in the stock, scraping the bottom of the pot to loosen any browned bits and rice. Rice grains should be under the level of the liquid. Pour the tomatoes over the top but do not stir. Close and lock the lid, making sure the steam release handle is in the sealing position.

Cook on high pressure for 4 minutes. When finished, release the pressure naturally for 10 minutes, then quickly release remaining steam by turning the handle to the venting position. Unlock the lid and open it carefully.

Fluff the rice with two forks and then stir in the reserved chicken and sausage. Replace the lid and let rest for about 4 minutes, or until the meats are heated through. Scoop into serving bowls, sprinkle the tops with chopped parsley, and serve hot.

NOTE:

Most recipes for jambalaya call for a "Cajun seasoning" mix. Unfortunately, many spice blends contain gluten or have cross-contamination issues. It may take a few minutes longer to make your own, but the payoff is better-tasting and safe-to-eat meals your whole family can enjoy.

Saffron Risotto

GLUTEN FREE • DAIRY-FREE OPTION • VEGETARIAN • VEGAN OPTION • SOY FREE • NUT FREE • EGG FREE

½ teaspoon saffron threads

3 tablespoons (45 ml) boiling water

1 tablespoon (15 ml) olive or vegetable oil

½ medium onion, finely chopped

1 clove garlic, minced

1½ cups (285 g) Arborio or Carnaroli rice (do not substitute another style of rice)

2 tablespoons (30 ml) gluten-free dry white wine (optional; see Note, page 51)

1¾ cups (415 ml) water

2 cups (470 ml) vegetable stock, divided

½ teaspoon kosher or fine sea salt

¼ teaspoon freshly ground black pepper

2 tablespoons (28 g) unsalted butter or dairy-free/vegan alternative such as Earth Balance

1 teaspoon freshly grated lemon zest (optional)

1 cup (150 g) frozen peas

Grated Parmesan cheese (optional, omit for dairy free and vegan)

—

4 servings

In a small bowl, soak the saffron in the hot water.

Press Sauté to heat the inner pot of your pressure cooker. Add the oil and heat until shimmering, then stir in the onion and garlic. Cook, stirring often, until the onion has softened slightly, about 4 minutes. Add the rice and stir to coat all the grains with the oil. Pour in the wine and cook until absorbed. Stir in the water, 1½ cups (355 ml) of the stock, the saffron with the soaking water, and the salt and pepper. Stir to make sure no browned bits are stuck on the bottom of the pot. Press Cancel.

Close and lock the lid, making sure the handle is in the sealing position. Cook for 4 minutes on high pressure. When it is finished, release the pressure naturally for 8 minutes, then turn the knob to the venting position and quickly release the remaining pressure. Unlock the lid and open it carefully.

Stir the rice until smooth and all the liquid has been incorporated. Stir in the butter until melted and the rice is creamy. Stir in the lemon zest and peas. Replace the lid and let the peas steam for 3 minutes. Taste and adjust the seasonings with more salt or pepper if needed. Toss the rice to evenly distribute the peas. If you want a creamier, looser texture, stir in the remaining ½ cup (120 ml) stock.

Ladle into bowls, sprinkle each with a little Parmesan cheese, if desired, and serve.

NOTE:

Saffron is a lovely, aromatic, and expensive spice. If you are looking for a less costly alternative, use ½ teaspoon turmeric in its place. Stir it into the rice after you've added the stock. It will add a pretty yellow hue and delicate flavor. It's not as fragrant as saffron, but still delicious.

Creamy Parmesan Brown Rice

GLUTEN FREE • DAIRY-FREE OPTION • VEGETARIAN • SOY FREE • NUT FREE • EGG FREE

2 tablespoons (30 ml) olive or vegetable oil

1 medium onion, finely diced

1 carrot, trimmed and finely diced

1 red bell pepper, seeded and finely diced

2 teaspoons (1 g) fresh thyme leaves or 1 teaspoon dried thyme

1 teaspoon dried oregano

1 cup (180 g) short-grain brown rice, such as Lundberg Family Farms brand

¼ cup (60 ml) gluten-free dry white wine or water (see Note, page 51)

1¼ cups (295 ml) vegetable stock or water, plus more if needed

½ teaspoon salt

¼ to ½ teaspoon freshly ground black pepper

¼ cup (35 g) frozen peas

½ cup (50 g) grated Parmesan or (60 g) Monterey Jack cheese or dairy-free cheese

—

4 servings

Press Sauté on your electric pressure cooker. Add the oil and heat until shimmering. Add the onion, carrot, and bell pepper and cook, stirring, until the onion is softened, about 3 minutes. Stir in the thyme and oregano, and then stir in the rice, making sure that all the grains are coated with the oil. Add the wine and cook until it is absorbed by the rice, stirring constantly. Be sure there are no browned bits stuck to the bottom of the pot. Pour in the stock and add the salt and pepper. Press Cancel.

Close and lock the lid, making sure the steam release handle is in the sealing position. Cook on high pressure for 23 minutes. When it is finished, release the pressure naturally for 12 minutes, then turn the steam release handle to venting. When the float pin drops, unlock the lid and open it carefully.

Stir the peas into the rice and sprinkle the Parmesan over the top. Replace the lid, and let rest for about 3 minutes to cook the peas and melt the cheese. If you want a creamier consistency, stir in a little more stock. Taste and adjust the seasonings if needed. Serve immediately.

Millet Tabbouleh

GLUTEN FREE • DAIRY FREE • VEGETARIAN • VEGAN • SOY FREE • NUT FREE • EGG FREE

FOR THE MILLET

1 cup (175 g) whole-grain millet, rinsed well and drained

2 cups (470 ml) cool water

1 teaspoon kosher or fine sea salt

FOR THE TABBOULEH

1 cup (100 g) minced scallion

¼ cup (24 g) finely chopped fresh mint leaves

¼ cup (15 g) finely chopped fresh flat-leaf parsley

1 cucumber, peeled, split lengthwise, and seeds scraped out, finely diced

2 cups (300 g) cherry tomatoes, quartered and drained in a strainer

1 teaspoon kosher or fine sea salt

½ teaspoon freshly ground black pepper

FOR THE DRESSING

¼ cup (60 ml) extra virgin olive oil

2 tablespoons (30 ml) freshly squeezed lemon juice

¼ to ½ teaspoon honey

¼ teaspoon kosher or fine sea salt

⅛ teaspoon freshly ground black pepper

—

4 to 6 servings

MILLET: Place the millet, water, and salt in the inner pot of your electric pressure cooker. Close and lock the lid, making sure the steam release handle is in the sealing position. Cook on high pressure for 9 minutes. When it is finished, release the pressure naturally for 10 minutes, then turn the steam release handle to venting, releasing any remaining steam. Unlock the lid and open it carefully.

If there is any excess water, pour the millet into a fine-mesh strainer to drain. Transfer to a large bowl and set aside to cool to room temperature, tossing and raking it occasionally with two forks to ensure it doesn't clump.

TABBOULEH: Add the scallions, mint, parsley, cucumbers, tomatoes, salt, and pepper to the millet. Toss to combine.

DRESSING: In a bowl, whisk together the oil and lemon juice until emulsified. Whisk in the honey, salt, and pepper. Taste and adjust the seasonings if needed, then drizzle half over the salad. Toss to coat everything with the dressing. Cover and let rest for at least 30 minutes before tasting and adjusting the seasonings. Add more dressing if desired. Serve at room temperature. Store, covered, in the refrigerator.

Brown and Wild Rice Pilaf with Mushrooms and Snow Peas

GLUTEN FREE • DAIRY FREE • VEGETARIAN • VEGAN • SOY FREE • NUT FREE • EGG FREE

2 tablespoons (30 ml) olive or vegetable oil, divided

1 shallot, thinly sliced

4 ounces (115 g) snow peas, strings removed, thinly sliced

6 large mushrooms, sliced

½ cup (75 g) dried sweetened cranberries

¼ cup (40 g) finely chopped onion

2 cups (360 g) brown and wild rice blend

½ cup (120 ml) gluten-free dry white wine or more stock (see Note, page 51)

1 cup (235 ml) vegetable stock, chicken stock, or water

1 cup (235 ml) water

½ teaspoon kosher or fine sea salt

½ teaspoon freshly ground black pepper

½ cup (55 g) sliced almonds

—

6 to 8 servings

Press Sauté on your pressure cooker and add 1 tablespoon (15 ml) of the oil to the inner pot. Add the shallots, snow peas, and mushrooms. Cook, stirring often, until the shallots are softened, about 2 minutes. Use a slotted spoon to transfer the vegetables to a bowl. Stir in the cranberries and set aside.

With the pressure cooker still on Sauté, pour the remaining 1 tablespoon (15 ml) oil in the inner pot. Add the onion and cook until softened, about 4 minutes. Add the rice and toss to coat each grain with the oil. Add the wine to the pot and scrape the bottom to loosen any browned bits. Add the stock, water, salt, and pepper, stirring. Close and lock the lid, making sure the steam release handle is in the sealing position. Cook on high pressure for half the time listed on the rice package, about 20 minutes.

When it is finished, release the pressure naturally, about 12 minutes. Turn the steam release handle to venting, releasing any remaining steam. When the float pin drops, unlock the lid and open it carefully.

Stir in the reserved vegetables and any accumulated juices, replace the lid, and let rest for about 4 minutes. When the vegetables are reheated, remove the lid and use a fork to fluff the rice and distribute the vegetables evenly. If there is excess liquid, leave it on Keep Warm or press Sauté (set to low) for a few minutes with the lid off and it will evaporate. Scoop portions onto plates, sprinkle with the almonds, and serve.

NOTE:

Although wine is considered gluten free, to be super careful for highly reactive people, look for winemakers that use only stainless steel tanks for aging their wines. There is a very rare possibility of contamination from casks that are sealed with gluten-containing ingredients.

Millet and Chicken Greek Salad

GLUTEN FREE • DAIRY-FREE OPTION • SOY FREE • NUT FREE • EGG FREE

FOR THE SALAD

2 tablespoons (30 ml) vegetable or olive oil

½ cup (80 g) very finely chopped onion

1 red bell pepper, cored, seeded, and very finely chopped

1 cup (175 g) millet, rinsed well and drained

½ teaspoon kosher or fine sea salt

½ teaspoon freshly ground black pepper

1 teaspoon dried oregano

1 cup (235 ml) water

¾ cup (180 ml) chicken stock or water

1½ cups (60 g) baby spinach leaves, rinsed very well, shaken dry

1 small cucumber, peeled and finely chopped

⅓ cup (35 g) chopped olives, preferably Kalamata

⅓ cup (50 g) quartered cherry tomatoes

½ small red onion, very thinly sliced

1½ cups (210 g) cooked chicken (see page 72), cut into small cubes or shredded, at room temperature

FOR THE DRESSING

⅓ cup (80 ml) extra virgin olive oil

2 tablespoons (30 ml) freshly squeezed lemon juice

1 to 2 tablespoons (15 to 30 ml) red wine vinegar, to taste

½ teaspoon kosher or fine sea salt

¼ teaspoon freshly ground black pepper

FOR TOPPING

2 tablespoons (6 g) finely chopped fresh parsley

¼ cup (38 g) crumbled feta cheese (optional)

—

About 4 servings

SALAD: Press Sauté and heat the vegetable oil in the inner pot of your electric pressure cooker. When it is shimmering, add the chopped onion and bell pepper and cook, stirring, for 4 minutes, or until the onion is slightly softened. Add the millet. Sprinkle with the salt, pepper, and oregano, then pour in the water and stock, stirring to be sure nothing is stuck to the bottom of the pot. Press Cancel.

Close and lock the lid, making sure the steam release handle is in the sealing position. Cook on high pressure for 9 minutes. When it is finished, release the pressure naturally for 8 minutes, then turn the steam release handle to venting, releasing any remaining steam. Unlock the lid and open it carefully.

(continued)

Remove the lid, rake the grains with a fork, and transfer to a large bowl. Add the spinach to the bowl, stir it into the millet, and let the steam wilt the greens. Set aside to cool to room temperature, tossing occasionally with forks to help keep the millet from clumping. When cooled, stir in the cucumber, olives, tomatoes, red onion, and chicken.

DRESSING: In a small bowl, whisk together the olive oil, lemon juice, vinegar, salt, and pepper. Pour half the dressing over the salad, tossing to coat all the ingredients. Taste and adjust the seasonings; add the remaining dressing if desired and toss again. Sprinkle the parsley and feta over the top and serve.

Plentiful Pasta

Recipes

Chicken Tetrazzini with Rotini
(page 60)

Luscious Mac and Cheese with Crispy Bacon

GLUTEN FREE • VEGETARIAN OPTION • SOY FREE • NUT FREE • EGG FREE

4 slices gluten-free bacon, chopped (optional, replace with 2 tablespoons [30 ml] oil for vegetarian)

½ small onion, grated

3¾ cups (880 ml) water

12 ounces (340 g) uncooked elbow macaroni, such as Barilla gluten-free brand

1½ teaspoons kosher or fine sea salt

1 (12-ounce, or 340 g) can evaporated milk (*not* sweetened condensed) or whole milk

1 teaspoon dry mustard powder

1 teaspoon black pepper

½ teaspoon nutmeg (optional)

24 ounces (672 g) shredded extra-sharp cheddar cheese

8 ounces (227 g) shredded fontina or Monterey Jack cheese

2 ounces (56 g) grated Parmesan cheese

Hot pepper sauce, to taste (optional) (Sriracha brand is gluten free)

—

About 4 servings

Press Sauté on your electric pressure cooker. When hot, add the bacon to the inner pot and cook, stirring, until crisp. Transfer to a paper towel–lined plate to cool. Remove all but 2 tablespoons (30 ml) of the fat from the inner pot. Add the onion and cook, stirring, until fully softened, about 5 minutes. Press Cancel.

Add the water, pasta, and salt to the inner pot. Stir and make sure the pasta is completely covered with the liquid. Close and lock the lid, making certain the steam release handle is in the sealing position. Cook on high pressure for 1 minute.

When it is finished, release the pressure naturally for 4 minutes, then slowly vent the remaining pressure by moving the handle between venting and sealing, letting out a little steam at a time. Use a hot pad to protect your hand. When all the steam is released, unlock the lid and open it carefully.

Test the pasta; it should be just tender and not too chewy. If it needs more time, set the lid back on the pressure cooker and let it rest for a few minutes.

Stir the milk, mustard powder, pepper, and nutmeg into the cooked pasta. Mix until evenly distributed. Add the cheeses, a little at a time, stirring until melted and creamy before adding more. Add a little hot pepper sauce if desired. If the sauce gets too thick, add ¼ cup (60 ml) hot water or more to thin. Taste and adjust the seasonings if needed. Crumble the bacon and sprinkle on top; serve immediately.

NOTE:

A general rule of thumb when cooking gluten-free pasta, like Barilla, in the pressure cooker is to cut the recommended cook time in half and then take another minute or two off. Do a controlled pressure release, which stops the cooking more quickly than a natural pressure release. If you are using another brand of pasta, the timing may be different, so try the recipe as written, and then make adjustments as needed.

Creamy Pesto Pasta

GLUTEN FREE • VEGETARIAN • SOY FREE • EGG FREE

8 ounces (227 g) rotini pasta, such as Barilla gluten-free brand

1 teaspoon kosher or fine sea salt

1 tablespoon (15 ml) olive or vegetable oil

¼ cup (60 g) gluten-free pesto sauce, such as Buitoni or Trader Joe's brands, or more to taste

8 ounces (227 g) mascarpone cheese

¼ cup (25 g) grated Parmesan cheese

1½ cups (355 ml) water for the bottom of the pot

—

2 to 3 servings

NOTE:

The timing for the pasta may change depending on the brand of pasta you use. See page 56 for details.

Place the pasta in the inner pot of your electric pressure cooker and add water to cover. Stir in the salt and add the olive oil to the water to help prevent sticking.

Close and lock the lid, making sure the steam release handle is in the sealing position. Cook on high pressure for 1 minute. When it is finished, release the pressure naturally for 4 minutes. Then hold the steam release handle halfway between sealing and venting (use a hot pad to protect your hand) until all the steam is released. Unlock the lid and open it carefully. Press Cancel. Pour the pasta into a colander and drain well.

In a large mixing bowl, stir together the pesto and mascarpone until smooth. Add the pasta to the pesto mixture and stir until all the pieces are evenly coated.

Butter a 7-inch (18-cm) round baking pan and line the bottom with parchment paper. Place the pesto-coated pasta in the pan. Sprinkle the Parmesan on top. Place a square of foil over the pan, crimping around the edges of the pan.

Wipe out the inner pot. Pour in 1½ cups (355 ml) water and place a trivet in the bottom. Set the pan on a sling (see page 11) and place it on the trivet. Close and lock the lid, making sure the steam release handle is in the sealing position. Cook on high pressure for 2 minutes. When it is finished, release the pressure naturally for 5 minutes, then quickly release the remaining steam. Unlock the lid and open it carefully. Press Cancel.

Lift the pan out of the pot and set it on a wire cooling rack. Carefully lift the foil off the pan. If you want some color on the top, slip the pan under the broiler for a few minutes until the cheese is bubbling and browned in spots. Let rest for 5 minutes before scooping out servings.

Shrimp and Pasta in a Lemon Cream Sauce

GLUTEN FREE • SOY FREE • NUT FREE • EGG FREE

FOR THE PASTA

12 ounces (340 g) penne pasta, such as Barilla gluten-free brand

1 teaspoon kosher or fine sea salt

Olive oil, for tossing

FOR THE SHRIMP

1 tablespoon (15 ml) olive or vegetable oil

1 medium shallot, minced

1½ pounds (680 g) raw medium shrimp, peeled and deveined

½ teaspoon minced fresh dill

Kosher or fine sea salt and freshly ground black pepper, to taste

FOR THE LEMON CREAM SAUCE

3 tablespoons (42 g) butter

1½ cups (355 ml) heavy cream or evaporated milk

1½ cloves garlic, peeled

2 teaspoons (10 ml) freshly squeezed lemon juice

2 teaspoons (4 g) finely grated lemon zest

1¼ cups (125 g) grated Parmesan cheese, divided

Salt and freshly ground black pepper, to taste

Finely chopped fresh Italian parsley or chives, for garnish

—

4 servings

PASTA: Place the pasta in the inner pot of your pressure cooker. Pour in enough water to cover the pasta by 1 inch (2.5 cm). Stir the pasta to make sure it doesn't stick to the bottom of the pan. Sprinkle the salt in the water. Close and lock the lid, making sure the steam release handle is in the sealing position. Cook on high pressure for 2 minutes.

When it is finished, release the pressure naturally for 3 minutes, then do a controlled release by turning the steam release handle to halfway between sealing and venting positions. Protect your hand with a hot pad. When all the steam has been released, press Cancel. Unlock the lid and open

NOTE:

Shrimp come in a variety of sizes, and each will take a different amount of time to cook. You want to cook them in batches so every piece touches the bottom of the pot. When both sides are pink and opaque, remove from the heat and place in a bowl. Continue cooking the remaining shrimp until they are all just done. Cover the bowl and the residual heat will finish cooking them through.

it carefully. Pour the pasta into a colander, drain it, and toss with a little oil to keep it from sticking together as it sits. Wipe out the inner pot.

SHRIMP: Press Sauté and heat the inner pot. Add the oil and when hot, stir in the shallot. Cook for about 1 minute, until just beginning to color. Add half the shrimp and dill, tossing to coat with the oil. Cook, stirring often, until the shrimp become opaque and turn pink on both sides, 1 to 2 minutes on each side, until just done. Sprinkle lightly with salt and pepper. Use a slotted spoon to scoop the shrimp out of the pot and add to the pasta; cover to keep warm. Repeat with the remaining shrimp and dill.

LEMON CREAM SAUCE: Add the butter to the inner pot, warming until fully melted. Whisk in the cream, garlic, lemon juice, and zest. Cook until warmed, whisking often to avoid scorching. Discard the garlic. Whisk in 1 cup (100 g) of the Parmesan cheese until smooth. Press Cancel. Taste and adjust the seasonings with salt and pepper if needed.

Add the pasta and shrimp to the sauce, tossing to thoroughly coat each piece. Replace the lid and let it rest for a couple of minutes, or until the pasta and shrimp are heated through. Add a splash of water if the sauce gets too thick.

To serve, scoop the pasta and shrimp into bowls and sprinkle the top of each serving with 1 tablespoon (6 g) of the remaining Parmesan cheese and a little parsley. Serve hot.

NOTE:

The timing for the pasta may change depending on the brand of pasta you use. See page 56 for details.

Chicken Tetrazzini with Rotini

GLUTEN FREE • SOY FREE • EGG FREE • NUT FREE

1 tablespoon (15 ml) olive oil

2 pounds (908 g) boneless, skinless chicken breasts, cut into bite-size pieces

2 tablespoons (28 g) unsalted butter

1 yellow onion, chopped

2 cloves garlic, minced

4¼ cups (1 L) chicken stock, divided

1 tablespoon (2 g) fresh thyme leaves

2 teaspoons (6 g) smoked paprika

1 cup (235 ml) milk

12 ounces (340 g) rotini pasta, such as Barilla gluten-free brand

6 ounces (168 g) cream cheese, softened and cut into pieces

1 cup (100 g) freshly grated Parmesan cheese, plus more for serving

1 cup (150 g) frozen peas

½ cup (35 g) sliced button mushrooms

½ cup (30 g) chopped fresh parsley, for garnish

—

About 4 servings

NOTE:

The timing for the pasta may change depending on the brand of pasta you use. See page 56 for details.

Press Sauté on your electric pressure cooker. When the inner pot is hot, add the olive oil. Add the chicken to the oil and brown lightly on each side. Remove the chicken from the pot and set aside.

Add the butter and onions to the pot. Sauté for 2 minutes, or until soft. Add the garlic and cook for an additional 30 seconds, until fragrant.

Add 1 cup (235 ml) of the chicken stock to the pot, scraping the bottom of the pot to deglaze it. Return the chicken to the pot. Add the remaining 3¼ cups (765 ml) stock, thyme, paprika, milk, and pasta.

Close and lock the lid, making sure the steam release handle is in the sealing position. Cook on high pressure for 5 minutes. When the cook time is finished, press Cancel. Do a quick pressure release by carefully moving the sealing handle to venting and allowing all the steam to escape. When the float pin drops, unlock the lid and open it carefully.

Add the cream cheese pieces and stir gently until all the cheese is melted and the sauce is smooth. Stir in the Parmesan, peas, and mushrooms. Return the lid to the pot and allow to sit in the residual heat for 2 to 4 minutes, or until the peas are warmed through. The sauce will thicken as it cools, so be sure to stir it well before serving.

To serve, place in pretty bowls and garnish with plenty of parsley on top and extra Parmesan if needed!

Vegetable Macaroni Salad

GLUTEN FREE • DAIRY FREE • VEGETARIAN • NUT FREE

12 ounces (340 g) elbow macaroni, such as Barilla gluten-free brand

Olive or vegetable oil

2½ teaspoons (15 g) kosher or fine sea salt, divided

½ to ¾ cup (120 to 180 ml) gluten-free Italian salad dressing, such as Girard's Olde Venice Italian Dressing

1 teaspoon sugar (optional)

½ teaspoon freshly ground black pepper

½ teaspoon onion powder

¼ teaspoon ground celery seed

3 scallions, trimmed and finely chopped

2 stalks celery, trimmed and finely chopped

2 red bell peppers, cored, seeded, and finely chopped

1 large cucumber, finely chopped

½ pint (150 g) cherry tomatoes, cut in half

½ cup (50 g) sliced black olives (Lindsay brand is gluten-free)

3 tablespoons (9 g) chopped fresh parsley

—

6 to 8 servings

NOTE:

The timing for the pasta may change depending on the brand of pasta you use. See page 56 for details.

Place the pasta in the inner pot of your electric pressure cooker. Add fresh water to cover the pasta by 1 inch (2.5 cm). Stir 2 teaspoons (12 g) of the salt into the water and make sure the pasta is not sticking to the bottom of the pot.

Close and lock the lid, with the steam release handle in the sealing position. Cook on high pressure for 1 minute. When it is finished, release the pressure naturally for 4 minutes, then turn the steam release handle to venting, releasing remaining steam. When the pressure valve drops, unlock the lid and open it carefully. Pour the pasta into a colander and rinse with cool water to stop the cooking, and then drain thoroughly. Transfer to a large mixing bowl.

In a bowl, whisk together the dressing, sugar (if using), ½ teaspoon salt, pepper, onion powder, and celery seed. Pour ½ cup (120 ml) over the pasta and stir in the vegetables and parsley, mixing until evenly distributed and everything is coated with the dressing. Taste and adjust the seasonings, adding more dressing if needed. Store in the refrigerator, covered, until ready to serve.

Pork Tenderloin Marsala and Penne Pasta

GLUTEN FREE • DAIRY FREE • SOY FREE • NUT FREE • EGG FREE

8 ounces (227 g) penne pasta, such as Barilla gluten-free brand

2 teaspoons (12 g) kosher or fine sea salt, plus more to taste

2 tablespoons (30 ml) olive or vegetable oil, divided, plus more for drizzling

1 (about 1½-pound, or 680 g) pork tenderloin

4 slices pancetta or bacon, chopped

1 small onion, finely chopped

1 clove garlic, minced

8 ounces (227 g) cremini or button mushrooms, stemmed and halved or quartered

¾ cup (180 ml) sweet Marsala wine (see Note, page 51) or chicken stock

¼ cup (60 ml) chicken stock

Several sprigs fresh thyme

2 tablespoons (16 g) cornstarch (see page 15 for more information on thickeners)

3 tablespoons (45 ml) cool water

Kosher salt and freshly ground black pepper, as needed

Minced fresh parsley, for garnish

—

3 to 4 servings

Place the penne in the inner pot of your electric pressure cooker. Fill the pot with fresh water to cover by 1 inch (2.5 cm). Stir to make sure the pasta isn't sticking to the bottom of the pan. Sprinkle the salt in the water. Close and lock the lid, making sure the steam release handle is in the sealing position. Cook on high pressure for 2 minutes. When it is finished, release the pressure naturally for 3 minutes, then do a controlled release by holding the handle halfway between the sealing and venting positions. Protect your hand with a hot pad. When all the steam has been released, press Cancel.

Unlock the lid and open it carefully. Pour the pasta into a colander and drain. Drizzle with a little oil and toss to keep it from sticking together as it sits. Set aside and stir occasionally.

Press Sauté and heat 1 tablespoon (15 ml) of the oil in the inner pot. When shimmering, add the pork tenderloin. Brown for about 3 minutes on each side. Transfer the pork to a plate and tent with foil to help keep warm.

Add the remaining 1 tablespoon (15 ml) oil to the pot. Stir in the pancetta and cook until slightly crispy, about 4 minutes, stirring often. Use a slotted spoon to transfer the pancetta to a bowl. Remove all but 2 tablespoons (30 ml) of the fat. Add the onion to the pot and cook for 3 minutes, stirring, until softened. Stir in the garlic, cook for 30 seconds, then stir in the mushrooms. Cook, stirring often, for 2 minutes.

Pour in the Marsala wine and chicken stock. Scrape the bottom of the pan to loosen any browned bits. Transfer the pork and its juices back to the pot, nestling it into the liquid. Sprinkle in the cooked pancetta. Close and lock the lid, making sure the steam release handle is in the sealing position.

NOTE:

The timing for the pasta may change depending on the brand of pasta you use. See page 56 for details.

Cook on high pressure for 5 minutes. When it is finished, release the pressure naturally for 7 minutes, then turn the steam release handle to venting, releasing remaining steam. Unlock the lid and open it carefully. Press Cancel. Remove the pork from the pot, check to make sure it has reached at least 145°F (63°C) in the center with an instant-read thermometer (if it needs more time, return it to the pot and let rest in the heat for a few minutes longer), place on a cutting board, cover, and keep warm.

Add the thyme to the pot. In a small bowl, whisk the cornstarch and water together until fully dissolved. Press Sauté and whisk the cornstarch slurry into the cooking liquid in the pot. Cook, whisking constantly, until it comes to a boil and thickens. Taste and adjust the seasonings with salt and pepper if needed.

Stir the pasta into the sauce and return the tenderloin to the pot. Replace the lid and let rest for 1 to 2 minutes to rewarm the pasta. Press Cancel.

Cut the pork into thick slices. Divide the pork between plates, add some of the pasta, top with the sauce and mushrooms, sprinkle with the parsley, and serve hot.

Classic Lasagna with Meat Sauce

GLUTEN FREE • SOY FREE • NUT FREE • EGG FREE

FOR THE MEAT SAUCE

1 tablespoon (15 ml) olive or vegetable oil

½ pound (227 g) ground beef

½ pound (227 g) ground pork (*not* sausage)

1 medium onion, finely chopped

2 cloves garlic, minced

2 cups (480 g) gluten-free crushed or strained tomatoes, such Pomi brand

1 tablespoon (3 g) dried oregano

¼ teaspoon whole fennel seeds

2 teaspoons (12 g) kosher or fine sea salt

½ teaspoon freshly ground black pepper

FOR THE CHEESE MIXTURE

1 cup (240 g) ricotta cheese

½ cup (50 g) grated Parmesan cheese

2 tablespoons (5 g) chopped fresh basil leaves

2 teaspoons (1 g) dried oregano

½ teaspoon kosher or fine sea salt

½ teaspoon freshly ground black pepper

FOR ASSEMBLY

½ (10-ounce, or 283 g) box oven-ready lasagna noodles, such as Barilla gluten-free brand

1½ cups (180 g) shredded mozzarella cheese

¼ cup (25 g) grated Parmesan cheese

Extra chopped basil leaves, for garnish

For the cooking pot

1½ cups (355 ml) water

—

About 4 servings

Line the bottom of a 7-inch (18 cm) round springform pan or push pan (like you use to make cheesecake) with parchment paper. Line the sides with a strip of parchment. Wrap the bottom of the pan with a sheet of foil to contain any liquids. Set aside.

MEAT SAUCE: Press Sauté on your electric pressure cooker. Add the oil to the inner pot and brown the meats. Use a spoon or flat-edged spatula to break up clumps, making the pieces as small as you can. Add the onion and garlic and cook, stirring, until the onion is softened, about 4 minutes. Stir in the tomatoes, oregano, fennel seeds, salt, and pepper. Simmer for about 5 minutes to blend the flavors. Taste the sauce and add more salt or pepper if needed. Pour into a bowl. Clean the inner pot.

CHEESE MIXTURE: In a bowl, stir together the ricotta cheese, Parmesan, basil, oregano, salt, and pepper with a fork until smooth.

ASSEMBLY: Cover the bottom of the prepared baking pan with a thin layer of sauce. Break the lasagna noodles to fit in a single layer in the bottom of the pan. Top with more of the sauce (enough to fully cover the pasta), half of the ricotta mixture, and one-third of the mozzarella. Repeat twice more, each time pressing down gently on the noodle layer to compress slightly before adding other ingredients. The final layer will be sauce and mozzarella. Sprinkle the top with the ¼ cup (25 g) Parmesan.

Spray a piece of foil with nonstick vegetable spray (without flour) and lay it, sprayed side down, loosely on top of the pan. Crimp the edges of the foil to keep the steam out of the pan.

Pour the water into the bottom of the inner pot. Place a trivet in the bottom. Using a sling, set the pan on the trivet. Close and lock the lid, making sure the steam release handle is in the sealing position. Cook on high pressure for 24 minutes. When it is finished, release the pressure naturally for 10 minutes, then turn the steam release handle to venting, releasing any remaining steam. Unlock the lid and open it carefully.

Lift the pan out of the pot, remove the foil, and check to see if it is done by inserting a knife in several places; it should meet no resistance. Set the pan on a baking sheet. If desired, place under the broiler to brown the cheese on top. Remove from the oven and set aside to rest for 10 minutes before cutting into servings, sprinkling a little chopped basil on top of each piece.

NOTE:

If you are using a push-pan instead of a springform, you will have fun. It is similar to a tart pan where the bottom is set into the pan. To remove the lasagna (or cheesecakes), place the pan onto a large can of tomatoes or similar heavy object. Then carefully press down on the sides of the pan, sliding it down and revealing the layers of the lasagna. When the sides are completely clear, lift the lasagna from its base and set on a cutting board before slicing into wedges and serving.

Masterful Main Dishes

Recipes

Vegetable Lasagna *(page 70)*

Chicken Tikka Masala

GLUTEN FREE • SOY FREE • NUT FREE

FOR THE SAUCE

1 teaspoon ground coriander

2 teaspoons (6 g) ground cumin

¼ teaspoon ground cardamom

1 teaspoon turmeric

1 teaspoon kosher salt

½ teaspoon freshly ground black pepper

¼ teaspoon cayenne pepper

1½ teaspoons smoked paprika

1 tablespoon (8 g) garam masala (Penzeys brand is gluten free)

1 tablespoon (8 g) grated peeled fresh ginger (from a 1-inch, or 2.5 cm, piece)

1½ cups (360 g) canned tomato puree

3 tablespoons (45 g) tomato paste

½ cup (120 ml) chicken stock

FOR THE CHICKEN

2 tablespoons (30 ml) olive oil

1½ pounds (680 g) boneless, skinless chicken thighs, cut into bite-size pieces

1 large onion, thinly sliced

½ cup (120 ml) chicken stock

FOR THE RICE

2 cups (348 g) jasmine rice (Lundberg Farms brand is gluten free)

1 tablespoon (14 g) unsalted butter

2¼ cups (530 ml) water

FOR FINISHING

2 teaspoons (6 g) garam masala (Penzeys brand is gluten free)

½ cup (120 ml) heavy cream

½ cup (8 g) chopped fresh cilantro, for garnish

—

4 servings

SAUCE: In a medium bowl, combine all the ingredients for the sauce. Set aside.

CHICKEN: Press Sauté on your electric pressure cooker. When the inner pot is hot, add the oil and brown the chicken pieces for 2 to 3 minutes per side. Remove the chicken to a plate when brown. You may need to do this in batches.

Add the onion to the pot and sauté for 3 minutes, until slightly soft. Pour in the chicken stock, scraping with a wooden spoon to get up any browned bits on the bottom of the pot. Press Cancel.

Pour the prepared sauce into the pot and stir to combine. Return the chicken to the pot and fully submerge in the sauce. Add a long-legged trivet to the pot over the chicken and sauce, making sure the legs of the trivet are touching the bottom of the pot.

RICE: Place the rice in a fine-mesh colander and rinse under cold water until the water runs clear, about 1 minute. Place the rinsed rice, butter, and water into a 7 x 3-inch (18 x 7.6 cm) cake pan. Cover the pan with foil, crimping well to seal the edges. Lower the rice pan on top of the trivet using a foil sling (see page 11).

Close and lock the lid, making sure the steam release handle is in the sealing position. Cook on high pressure for 15 minutes. When the cook time is finished, do a quick pressure release by carefully moving the sealing handle to venting and allowing all the steam to escape. When the float pin drops, unlock the lid and open it carefully. Press Cancel.

FINISHING: Remove the rice pan from the cooking pot and set aside. Press Sauté. Add the garam masala to the liquid in the pot and simmer for 10 minutes to thicken, stirring often. Add the heavy cream and heat through, 2 more minutes.

Serve the chicken in big bowls with the rice and masala sauce, garnished with cilantro.

NOTE:

If you don't like cilantro, substitute flat-leaf parsley or chopped scallion.

Vegetable Lasagna

GLUTEN FREE • VEGETARIAN • SOY FREE • NUT FREE

- 1 tablespoon (15 ml) olive oil
- 1 medium onion, diced
- 4 cloves garlic, minced
- 1 teaspoon red pepper flakes
- 2 cups (140 g) sliced button mushrooms
- 1 cup (120 g) finely diced carrot
- 1 cup (150 g) finely diced red bell pepper
- 1½ cups (355 ml) water
- 1 cup (240 g) low-fat ricotta cheese or small-curd cottage cheese
- 1½ cups (180 g) part-skim mozzarella cheese, divided
- 1 cup (100 g) grated Parmesan cheese, divided
- 1 egg
- 1 tablespoon (6 g) dried oregano
- 1 teaspoon dried parsley
- 6 to 9 no-boil, oven-ready lasagna noodles, such as Barilla gluten-free brand
- 3 cups (750 g) your favorite gluten-free marinara sauce
- ¼ cup (10 g) chopped fresh basil leaves
- 2 medium zucchini, thinly sliced lengthwise

—

4 servings

Press Sauté on your electric pressure cooker. When the inner pot is hot, add the oil and onion. Cook for 2 to 3 minutes, or until the onion begins to soften. Add the garlic and red pepper flakes and cook for an additional 30 seconds, until the garlic is fragrant.

Add the mushrooms, carrot, and bell pepper to the pot. Cook for another 2 minutes. Remove the sautéed vegetables to a medium bowl. Drain any excess liquids. Set aside.

Rinse your pot and dry well, inside and out. Return the inner pot to the body of your pressure cooker. Place a trivet in the bottom of the pot and add the water. Spray a 7 x 3-inch (18 x 7.6 cm) push pan or round cake pan with nonstick cooking spray.

In a small bowl, combine the ricotta cheese, 1 cup (120 g) of the mozzarella cheese, ½ cup (50 g) of the Parmesan cheese, egg, oregano, and parsley. Set aside.

Break 3 pasta pieces and arrange them evenly in the bottom of the pan. A little bit of overlap is fine. Spread 1 cup (250 g) of the marinara sauce over the noodles. Layer half of the chopped basil over the sauce. Add half of the zucchini slices and spread

NOTE:

The pan you use for this recipe should be at least 3 inches (7.6 cm) deep. Anything less won't fit all the delicious vegetable and cheese layers.

half of the drained vegetable mixture over the slices. Spread half of the cheese mixture over the vegetables, spreading as evenly as possible.

Repeat with another layer of pasta, sauce, basil, zucchini, vegetables, and cheese. Top with the remaining 3 pasta sheets and remaining 1 cup (250 g) tomato sauce. Sprinkle the remaining ½ cup (60 g) mozzarella and remaining ½ cup (50 g) Parmesan cheese on top.

Cover the pan with aluminum foil, crimping the edges to seal. Using a foil sling (see page 11), lower the lasagna pan onto the trivet.

Close and lock the lid, making sure the steam release knob is in the sealing position. Cook on high pressure for 20 minutes. When the cook time is finished, allow a 10-minute natural release, then turn the knob to the venting position, releasing any remaining steam. When the float pin drops, unlock the lid and open it carefully.

Allow the lasagna to sit for a few minutes to set, then carefully remove it from the pan.

NOTES:

The timing for the pasta may change depending on the brand of pasta you use. See page 56 for details.

The Barilla lasagna noodles fit perfectly into a 7-inch (18-cm) round pan, but if you stack three sheets overlapping like the spokes of a wheel, they may not fully cook through in the center. Break them into smaller pieces and arrange in a jigsaw pattern, slightly overlapping.

Classic Whole Baked Chicken

GLUTEN FREE • DAIRY FREE • SOY FREE • EGG FREE • NUT FREE

1 (3- to 5-pound, or 1362 to 2270 g) whole chicken

1 tablespoon (18 g) salt, divided

1 lemon, cut in half

1 onion, cut into quarters

2 teaspoons (4 g) freshly ground pepper

2 teaspoons (4 g) paprika

1 teaspoon dried thyme

1 cup (235 ml) water

Oil or melted unsalted butter (optional, for crisping skin)

—

4 servings

NOTE:

Make sure your chicken fits easily inside the inner pot of your pressure cooker. Some whole chickens might be too large.

Remove any giblets or other innards from the cavity of the chicken. Pat dry with a paper towel. Sprinkle 1 teaspoon (6 g) of the salt inside the chicken. Place the cut lemon and onion pieces inside the chicken cavity. Sprinkle the remaining 2 teaspoons (12 g) salt, pepper, paprika, and thyme evenly over the chicken.

Put a trivet in the inner pot of your electric pressure cooker and add the water. Place the seasoned chicken, with the breast facing up, on top of the trivet.

Close and lock the lid, making sure the steam release knob is in the sealing position. Cook on high pressure for 6 minutes per pound (454 g).

3-pound (1.4 kg) chicken = 18 minutes
4-pound (1.8 kg) chicken = 24 minutes
5-pound (2.3 kg) chicken = 30 minutes

If your chicken is between weights, add 3 minutes for every half pound (227 g).

EXAMPLE: One 4½-pound (2 kg) chicken would equal 27 minutes on high pressure.

When the cooking time is finished, allow a natural release for 20 minutes, then move the pressure release knob to the venting position and release any remaining steam. When the float pin drops, unlock the lid and open it carefully.

If you like your chicken skin crispy, after removing it from the pot, transfer to a foil-lined baking sheet. Brush with oil or melted butter and place under the broiler for 2 to 4 minutes.

Southwestern Meatloaf

DAIRY FREE • SOY FREE • NUT FREE • EGG FREE

1 tablespoon (15 ml) olive or vegetable oil

½ large onion, very finely chopped

2 stalks celery, very finely chopped

2 carrots, very finely chopped

1 red bell pepper, cored, seeded, and very finely chopped

1 pound (454 g) lean ground beef

1 tablespoon (15 ml) Worcestershire sauce

2 teaspoons (1 g) chopped fresh cilantro

2 teaspoons (4 g) gluten-free ancho chile powder or chili powder

1 teaspoon kosher or fine sea salt

1 teaspoon ground cumin

½ teaspoon freshly ground black pepper

¼ teaspoon garlic powder (*not* garlic salt)

¼ cup (60 ml) barbecue sauce

1 cup (60 ml) water for the bottom of the pot

—

4 servings

NOTES:

To brown the top of the meatloaf, slide it under the broiler for a few minutes, once it's on the baking sheet.

Press Sauté on your electric pressure cooker. When the inner pot is hot, add the oil. Add the onion, celery, carrots, and pepper and cook, stirring often, until the onion has softened, 3 to 5 minutes. Press Cancel. Remove the inner pot from the machine and set aside to cool slightly.

In a bowl, combine the meat with the Worcestershire and seasonings until evenly coated. Fold in the cooled vegetables. When evenly distributed, pat the meat into a mounded disk about 6 inches (15 cm) in diameter and place in a 7-inch (18-cm) round baking pan. Brush the barbecue sauce over the top of the loaf. Cover the pan with foil. Wipe out the inner pot.

Place a trivet in the bottom of the inner pot and pour in the water. Set the meatloaf onto a rack with handles or a foil sling (see page 11) and lower onto the trivet. Close and lock the lid, making sure the steam release handle is in the sealing position. Cook on high pressure for 22 minutes, or until an instant-read thermometer registers at least 160°F (71°C) when inserted into the center of the meatloaf.

When it is finished, release the pressure naturally for 8 minutes, then release the rest of the pressure by moving the handle to the venting position. Unlock the lid and open it carefully.

Lift the sling out of the inner pot, carefully remove the foil from the pan, and transfer the meatloaf to a baking sheet.

Cut into slices to serve and pass additional barbecue sauce at the table.

Steamed Salmon and Garlic Red Potatoes

GLUTEN FREE • NUT FREE • SOY FREE • EGG FREE

4 tablespoons (56 g) unsalted butter, divided

1 cup (235 ml) chicken stock

1 pound (454 g) small red-skinned potatoes, quartered

1 large onion, cut into 8 wedges

1 teaspoon salt, divided

1 teaspoon freshly ground black pepper, divided

4 (5- to 6-ounce, or 140 to 168 g, each) skin-on center-cut salmon fillets (¾ to 1 inch, or 1.8 to 2.5 cm, thick)

1 teaspoon grated lemon zest

2 tablespoons (20 g) minced garlic

3 cups (105 g) baby spinach

1 tablespoon (2 g) fresh thyme leaves

1 tablespoon (2 g) fresh rosemary leaves, minced

Lemon wedges, for serving

—

4 servings

NOTE:

Use salmon with the skin attached. It will help hold the fillet together as it cooks.

Press Sauté on your electric pressure cooker. When the inner pot is hot, add 3 tablespoons (42 g) of the butter. Once the butter has melted, press Cancel.

Pour the chicken stock into the pot with the butter. Add the potatoes and onion wedges. Sprinkle ½ teaspoon each of the salt and pepper over the vegetables. Place a long-legged trivet over the potatoes and onions. Place an expandable steamer basket on top of the trivet.

Season the salmon fillets generously with the lemon zest and remaining ½ teaspoon each salt and pepper. Place skin side down on the steamer basket.

Close and lock the lid, making sure the steam release handle is in the sealing position. Cook on high pressure for 3 minutes. When the cook time is finished, do a quick pressure release by carefully moving the sealing handle to venting and allowing all the steam to escape. When the float pin drops, unlock the lid and open it carefully. Press Cancel.

Remove the salmon and place on a serving tray; tent lightly with foil to keep warm. Remove the steamer basket and trivet. Drain the potatoes and onions, reserving ¼ cup (60 ml) of the cooking liquid. Return the vegetables to the pot, along with the reserved cooking liquid.

Press Sauté. When the potatoes start sizzling, add the garlic and cook, stirring, until softened, 1 to 2 minutes; stir in the remaining 1 tablespoon (14 g) butter and additional salt and pepper if desired.

Press Cancel. Add the spinach, thyme, and rosemary to the potatoes and stir until the greens are wilted.

Divide the potato/spinach mixture equally among 4 plates. Top the greens with the salmon and serve with lemon wedges.

Chicken Pot Pie Casserole

GLUTEN FREE • SOY FREE • NUT FREE

2 tablespoons (30 ml) vegetable oil

1½ pounds (680 g) boneless, skinless chicken breasts, cut into bite-size cubes

1 teaspoon salt

2 teaspoons (6 g) pepper

1 medium onion, diced

1 tablespoon (10 g) minced garlic

1 cup (150 g) frozen peas and carrots

½ cup (75 g) frozen green beans

½ cup (75 g) frozen corn kernels

12 ounces (340 g) linguini noodles, such as Barilla gluten-free brand, broken in half

3¼ cups (765 ml) chicken stock

2 tablespoons (4 g) fresh thyme leaves

¾ cup (180 ml) heavy cream

—

8 servings

NOTE:

The timing for the pasta may change depending on the brand of pasta you use. See page 56 for details.

Press Sauté on your electric pressure cooker. When the inner pot is hot, add the oil. Generously season the chicken pieces with the salt and pepper. Add to the oil. Sauté for 2 to 3 minutes per side until the outside of the chicken is white. Remove the chicken from the pan.

Add the onion to the pan and sauté until soft but not brown, 2 to 3 minutes. Add the garlic and cook an additional 30 seconds, until fragrant. Press Cancel.

Return the chicken to the pot and add the frozen vegetables, linguini noodles, chicken stock, and thyme.

Close and lock the lid, making sure the steam release handle is in the sealing position. Press Manual and cook on high pressure for 6 minutes.

When the cook time is finished, do a quick pressure release and allow all the steam to escape. When the float pin drops, unlock the lid and open it carefully. Press Cancel.

Stir in the heavy cream. Press Sauté. Allow the mixture to cook for another 2 to 3 minutes, or until it thickens to your desired consistency.

Beef Short Ribs and Mushrooms with Red Wine Sauce

GLUTEN FREE • DAIRY FREE • NUT FREE • SOY FREE

2 tablespoons (30 ml) olive or vegetable oil

3 pounds (1362 g) bone-in beef short ribs, cut into smaller pieces

1 medium onion, chopped

2 carrots, chopped

2 stalks celery, chopped

1 large bell pepper, cored and chopped

2 poblano peppers, chopped

½ cup (120 ml) gluten-free dry red wine (see Note, page 51)

1 cup (235 ml) beef stock

2 tablespoons (30 ml) balsamic vinegar

2 tablespoons (30 g) tomato paste

5 sprigs fresh or 4 teaspoons (2 g) dried thyme

2 sprigs fresh or 2 teaspoons (1 g) dried rosemary

2 bay leaves

Kosher or fine sea salt and freshly ground black pepper, to taste

2 tablespoons (30 ml) cool water

1 tablespoon (8 g) cornstarch or 1½ tablespoons (12 g) potato starch (*not* potato flour)

8 ounces (227 g) small white or cremini mushrooms, cleaned and quartered

—

3 to 4 servings

Press Sauté on your electric pressure cooker. Pour the oil into the inner pot. When the oil is hot, add half the ribs and brown well on both sides. Transfer to a platter and repeat with the remaining ribs. Add the vegetables to the pot and cook, stirring often, until the onions are translucent, about 5 minutes.

In a large measuring cup, stir together the wine, beef stock, balsamic vinegar, and tomato paste. When the paste is dissolved, pour the mixture into the pot and scrape the bottom. Stir in the herbs and seasonings. Press Cancel. Return the ribs to the pot.

Close and lock the lid, making sure the steam release handle is in the sealing position before cooking on high pressure for 35 to 40 minutes, depending on rib size. When the time is up, let the pressure naturally release for 15 minutes, then turn the steam release handle to venting and release any remaining steam. Press Cancel. Unlock the lid and open it carefully.

Transfer the ribs to a clean platter. Pour the cooking liquid through a fat separator, straining out the solids, and pour the juices back into the pot, leaving the fat behind. Press Sauté and bring the liquid to a boil. Cook, whisking often, for about 5 minutes to reduce the sauce.

In a small bowl, whisk together the water and cornstarch until smooth. Stir the resulting slurry into the sauce, whisking constantly, until thickened. Taste and adjust the seasonings with salt and pepper. Press Cancel.

Return ribs to the sauce. Stir in the mushrooms, replace the lid, and let sit for 5 to 8 minutes. Serve the ribs drizzled with the sauce.

Tacos al Pastor with Pineapple Salsa

GLUTEN FREE • DAIRY FREE • SOY FREE • NUT FREE • EGG FREE

FOR THE PORK FILLING

2 tablespoons (30 ml) vegetable oil

3 to 4 pounds (1362 to 1816 g) boneless pork shoulder, visible fat trimmed, cut into 2-inch (5 cm) cubes

1 cup (165 g) pineapple chunks, well drained, cut into small pieces

1 small red onion, minced

1½ cups (355 ml) orange juice or water

Juice of 2 limes

3 tablespoons (24 g) chili powder

1 tablespoon (8 g) chipotle powder

1 teaspoon garlic powder (*not* garlic salt)

1 teaspoon ground cumin

1 teaspoon kosher or fine sea salt

1 teaspoon freshly ground black pepper

FOR THE PINEAPPLE SALSA

1½ cups (248 g) fresh pineapple cubes (if you cannot find fresh pineapple, use canned pineapple packed in water and drain well)

1 red bell pepper, seeded and finely chopped

½ small red onion, finely chopped

1 to 2 jalapeño peppers, seeded and minced

Juice of 1 to 2 limes, to taste

1 tablespoon (15 ml) olive oil

Chopped fresh cilantro, to taste

Sea salt and freshly ground black pepper, to taste

FOR ASSEMBLY

Gluten-free corn tortillas, such as Mission brand (see Note, page 36)

Chopped fresh cilantro (optional)

—

8 to 10 servings

PORK: Press Sauté on your pressure cooker and add the oil to the inner pot. When the oil is hot, add a portion of the pork cubes, and brown on all sides. Use a slotted spoon to transfer the meat to a plate and repeat with the remaining pork, working in batches. When it is all browned, place all the meat in the inner pot and add the pineapple, onion, orange and lime juices, chili and chipotle powders, garlic powder, and cumin. Stir to be sure there is nothing stuck to the bottom of the pot.

Close and lock the lid, making sure the steam release handle is in the sealing position. Cook on high pressure for 45 minutes. When it is finished, release the pressure naturally for 10 minutes, then quick release the remaining steam by moving the handle to venting. Unlock the lid and open it carefully.

Use a slotted spoon to transfer the pork to a large bowl. Use two forks to shred or cut into bite-size cubes. Pour 1 to 2 cups (235 to 470 ml) of the cooking liquid over the pork to keep it moist. Add the salt and pepper, taste, and adjust the seasonings.

PINEAPPLE SALSA: In a bowl, combine the pineapple, bell pepper, onion, jalapeños, lime juice, olive oil, and cilantro. Taste and add salt and pepper as desired. Can be made a day or two in advance.

ASSEMBLY: Fill the corn tortillas with the pork filling and add the pineapple salsa on top. Sprinkle with additional chopped cilantro, if desired, and serve.

Mom's Old-Fashioned Pot Roast

DAIRY FREE • SOY FREE • NUT FREE • EGG FREE

1 (3-pound, or 1.4 kg) boneless chuck roast

¾ teaspoon kosher or fine sea salt

½ teaspoon freshly ground black pepper

2 tablespoons (30 ml) olive oil

2 cups (470 ml) beef stock

½ cup (120 ml) dry red wine or water (see Note, page 51)

1 large onion, coarsely chopped

1 clove garlic, minced

2 bay leaves

1 teaspoon dried rosemary leaves

3 large russet potatoes, peeled and cut into large chunks

4 large carrots, trimmed and cut into large chunks

¼ cup (60 ml) cool water

2 tablespoons (16 g) cornstarch or potato starch

⅓ cup (50 g) frozen peas (optional)

2 tablespoons (6 g) finely chopped fresh parsley

—

4 to 6 servings

Pat the meat dry with paper towels and season with the salt and pepper. Press Sauté and pour the oil into the inner pot. When the oil is shimmering, add the meat and brown on both sides, about 5 minutes per side. Add the stock and wine, stirring to release any browned bits on the bottom of the pan. Stir in the onion, garlic, bay leaves, and rosemary. Press Cancel.

Close and lock the lid, making sure the steam release handle is in the sealing position. Cook on high pressure for 70 minutes. When it is finished, allow the pot to naturally release the pressure for 12 minutes, then turn the steam release handle to venting, releasing any remaining steam. Unlock the lid and open it carefully.

Quickly add the potatoes and carrots to the pot, replace the lid, set the steam release handle to sealing, bring back to pressure, and cook on high pressure for 3 minutes. Move the handle to venting and release the steam. Unlock the lid and open it carefully.

Using a slotted spoon and tongs, transfer the meat and vegetables to a platter. Discard the bay leaves and tent with foil to keep warm. Press Cancel.

In a small bowl, whisk together the water and cornstarch. While whisking, slowly pour the cornstarch slurry into the cooking liquid until fully blended. Press Sauté and bring the liquid in the pot to a boil, whisking constantly. Cook until thickened, about 1 minute, then taste and adjust the seasonings if needed. Press Cancel.

Stir in the peas, then return the meat and vegetables to the pot, stirring into the sauce. Place the lid on the pot and let sit for 4 minutes, or until peas are thawed and the meat is heated through. Scoop the meat and vegetables into bowls with some of the sauce, sprinkle with the chopped parsley, and serve.

NOTES:

Some people like tomato in their pot roast cooking liquid. If you want, you can whisk 2 tablespoons (30 g) tomato paste concentrate into the stock before adding the aromatics and seasonings.

Tender BBQ Pulled Pork with Ranch Slaw

GLUTEN FREE • NUT FREE

FOR THE PORK

3 tablespoons (45 ml) olive or vegetable oil

2 tablespoons (16 g) smoked paprika

2 tablespoons (25 g) brown sugar

1 tablespoon (8 g) chili powder (Penzeys and McCormick have gluten-free offerings)

2 teaspoons (1 g) dried oregano

1 teaspoon ground cumin

1 teaspoon kosher or fine sea salt

½ teaspoon black pepper

½ teaspoon onion powder

¼ teaspoon garlic powder

4 pounds (1816 g) boneless pork shoulder or butt, cut into large chunks

2 cups (470 ml) chicken stock

1 bell pepper, seeded and chopped

1 small onion, chopped

1 to 2 cups (235 to 470 ml) barbecue sauce (Stubb's entire line is gluten free, pick your favorite)

FOR THE DRESSING

1 cup (235 ml) low-fat buttermilk

½ cup (120 g) low-fat mayonnaise

1 teaspoon freshly squeezed lemon juice

¼ teaspoon very finely minced garlic

2 teaspoons (1 g) minced fresh chives

½ teaspoon dry mustard powder

1½ teaspoons thyme leaves

¼ teaspoon dried dill weed

Kosher or fine sea salt and black pepper, to taste

FOR THE SLAW

1 medium head green cabbage, preferably Napa cabbage, thinly sliced

Kosher salt

1 red bell pepper, cored and finely chopped

3 carrots, peeled and shredded

½ small red onion, very finely chopped

FOR SERVING

Gluten-free hamburger buns or sliced bread, such as Udi's brand

—

8 to 10 servings

PORK: In a bowl, combine the oil, paprika, brown sugar, chili powder, oregano, cumin, salt, pepper, onion powder, and garlic powder to make a paste. Smear over all sides of the pieces of pork. Pour the chicken stock into the inner pot and add the bell pepper and onion. Nestle the pork pieces into the liquid.

Close and lock the lid, making sure the steam release handle is in the sealing position. Cook on high pressure for 60 minutes. When it is finished, release the pressure naturally for 14 minutes, then turn the steam release handle to venting, releasing any remaining steam. When the float pin drops, unlock the lid and open it carefully.

Use a slotted spoon to transfer the pork, onions, and bell pepper to a baking sheet with sides. Reserve the cooking liquid. Use two forks to shred the meat, discarding large pieces of fat.

Pour the barbecue sauce into a bowl and add a little of the cooking liquid to thin slightly. Pour this mixture over the shredded pork, tossing to coat all the pieces. Transfer to a saucepan and keep warm over low heat, covered, stirring regularly. Add a little more of the cooking juices if the mixture starts to dry out.

This is also great made ahead. Refrigerate, covered, for a few days or freeze for longer storage.

DRESSING: In a medium bowl, combine the buttermilk, mayonnaise, and lemon juice. Whisk in the garlic, chives, mustard, thyme, and dill. Cover and refrigerate for at least 2 hours to give the flavors time to blend. Taste and adjust the seasonings with salt and pepper as desired.

SLAW: Place the sliced cabbage in a colander and liberally sprinkle with kosher salt. Toss gently to distribute the salt. Place the colander over a large bowl and set aside for 30 to 45 minutes. The salt will leach out most of the water, leaving the cabbage crispier. Rinse the cabbage well under cool running water, making sure the salt has been removed. Set the colander aside again to drain thoroughly, shaking it occasionally.

Transfer the drained cabbage to a very large mixing bowl and add the bell pepper, carrots, and onion. Toss to evenly distribute the ingredients and add ½ to ¾ cup (120 to 180 ml) of the dressing, tossing to evenly coat everything. Taste and adjust the seasonings as desired. Cover and refrigerate for at least 30 minutes. If any extra liquid accumulates while it is resting, drain before serving.

SERVE: Lightly toast the gluten-free hamburger buns if you like. Pile on some of the pulled pork and top with the slaw. Serve immediately.

NOTES:

To convert this to Hawaiian Kalua Pork, combine ¾ cup (180 ml) water mixed with 2 teaspoons (10 ml) liquid smoke (Wright's brand is gluten free) and 2 tablespoons (25 g) brown sugar in the bottom of the inner pot. Cut the pork into chunks, place in the pot, and sprinkle with 1 tablespoon (18 g) Alaea Red Hawaiian Sea Salt or 1½ teaspoons kosher salt. Cook on high pressure for 60 minutes with a 15-minute natural release. Shred the pork and add a little of the cooking liquid, tossing to combine. Serve with white rice (page 44) and a mango salsa.